"Build Your Brand Mania is a must read for any business person who delivers services and wants to expand their online reach to connect with clients that need and value their services. I highly recommend reading this book whether you have been in business 30 days or 30 years."

Manfred Sternberg // Attorney at Law
Manfred Sternberg & Assoc. PC

" 'Build Your Brand Mania' is a wonderful book delivering on its title, how to create the perfect following and customer base through online mechanisms. Too often the business owner relies on word-of-mouth to grow a business, which works, however, it takes generations to grow. Matt does a great job at educating each area and then provides detailed step-by-step instructions to implement the education."

Doug Winne, PMP, MG100 // Profit Strategist
ActionCOACH - Certified Million Dollar Coach

"As sales reps, we are always trying to differentiate ourselves from our competition and build a stronger relationship with prospects and clients. If you are looking for a way to build your brand, look no further! This book provides the strategies you need to stand out in today's world!"

Britney Owen // Regional Sales Manager
Global Chemical Distributor

"If you are contemplating how to tap into the internet to harness its power for your business or your innovations, 'Build Your Brand Mania' is your ticket! Matt Bertram systematically unveils the mysteries of saddling up and harnessing the World Wide Web for the common user! A must-have for any current or hopeful entrepreneur! Fresh information and ideas from a technology that's always evolving! Launch your future with this book!"

Mike Houston // Business Development
Star Home Health

"Matt's approach to business has always impressed me! He seems to always know just what his clients need and how to get them to that next level. He does it again with this book! He takes the complicated process of SEO and makes it relatable for anyone that wants to grow their business online."

Debbie Papp, CPA // Owner
The Window Center

BUILD YOUR
BRAND
MANIA

How to Transform Yourself Into an Authoritative
Brand That Will Attract Your Ideal Customers

Matt Bertram

Ainsley&Allen
PUBLISHING

Ainsley & Allen Publishing LLC
2035 Sunset Lake Road
Newark, DE 19702
www.ainsleyallenpublishing.com

Build Your Brand Mania – 1st ed.

ISBN-13: 978-1-946694-04-1
ISBN-13: 1-946694-04-5

Library of Congress Control Number: 2018949419

Dedicated to all the people that seek opportunity...
not security.

Table of Contents

Foreword

by Chris Burres

I wish this book existed when I started eWebResults back in 1999. Back then I was not yet an internet marketing expert. Of course, there weren't many internet marketing experts at all back in 1999. As I read this book, I saw the parallels in my history with eWebResults, similarities with how I had built my personal brand and the impact this had on my company's brand and success.

Some of the options mentioned in this book were not available when I started. There was no Facebook! MySpace had not yet come and gone. There was no LinkedIn. But the processes presented in this book, *Build Your Brand Mania*, of becoming "A Trusted Advisor" to businesses around the country and the world are the same processes I followed. My path to developing my brand began in 2009 when I started our podcast, "The SEO Podcast Unknown Secrets of Internet Marketing." Matt is now the co-host of this podcast with me.

Fundamentally, I believe the secret to my success is rooted in not only being a World Class Expert at internet marketing, but in building my personal brand. This book outlines the process for becoming that expert and how to build your brand.

If you're not an expert yet, don't worry. Becoming an industry-leading expert is straightforward and can be achieved by investing the time to truly understand your subject matter. Then, most importantly, you must teach and train people on the subject. Because it is when you teach a subject, you will truly understand it. Our podcast is the podium from which we teach internet marketing and the launching pad for the mania that has led us to be so successful.

Matt is a great friend and colleague. Not only is he one of the best marketers I have ever met, but he also works tirelessly to deliver value. We were in the middle of restructuring a company from the ground up when he asked me to write this Foreword. I told him I would be honored. In my head, I was thinking I would have a lot of time to prepare since I was sure it would take him a long time to write the book. Imagine my surprise a few weeks later when I received an email "Advanced copy of book" from Matt Bertram. My jaw dropped. "How?" I thought to myself. How in the middle of a company restructuring (that was going very well I might add) did Matt write a book?! We were in the middle of 70+ hour work weeks and he managed to write a book. Did I mention Matt works tirelessly to deliver value?

Part of me wanted to believe the book would need some work if you know what I mean. I had personally written zero books, but it was on my "to do" list. But, having worked with Matt and seeing what a machine he is when it comes to delivering results for customers, communicating with customers, finding, hiring, and training internet marketing experts… Deep down, I knew this was going to be an amazing book. I knew that what we were doing together in the restructuring came very naturally to him and he put that same knowledge, experience, and expertise into this book.

I only wish I had the benefit of reading Matt's book as I was building eWebResults. With the knowledge provided by this book, I am sure my journey would have been much more linear, and happened much, much faster. This is the age of **fast.** Everything feels faster now – because everything **is** faster now.

Read this book, apply what's inside, re-read the book, and you will build your brand even faster than I did. I wish you great success in your own journey!

Chris Burres
Co-Host "Unknown Secrets of Internet Marketing" SEO Podcast
Co-Founder of eWebResults

Foreword
by Brian Ainsley Horn

I've spent the last 10+ years helping entrepreneurs position themselves as authorities in their markets and create powerful brand experiences for their customers.

Achieving the "Trusted Advisor Status" like Matt outlines in this book ain't easy. Nothing about it is. But it's become more important than ever, because if you aren't a "Trusted Advisor", you are selling nothing more than a commodity like iron ore, sugar or rice.

The techniques Matt shares with you in this book are very powerful, and I want to make sure you are clear on the purpose of it, and will only use them to truly help your prospects and new found customers. I encourage you to take notes, listen to gems he shares and follow his outline. He knows what he is talking about.

Start *Building Your Brand Mania* with this book. Not tomorrow, not next week, or not when things get easier or you have more free time. That time will never come. Start today!

Brian Ainsley Horn
Co-Founder, Authority Alchemy

Acknowledgements

Jesus, who has saved my soul, thank you!

To my parents who played Robert Kiyosaki's "Cashflow" board game with me all those times in high school. It forever changed the course of my life.

Kristin, my wife for all the encouragement and allowing me to work all those late nights knowing it would be worth the sacrifice.

Chris and Brian for all your wisdom, guidance, and friendship.

To all my family, friends and colleagues that listened to all my crazy ideas and believed in me.

Introduction

Do you want more customers right now? I can't think of any business owner or entrepreneur who doesn't!

As a seasoned business owner, you probably already know what it takes to make that happen. You need to generate leads, qualify those leads as real prospects, and then turn those prospects into customers.

You also probably know a handful of extremely successful business owners in your field who are accomplishing this by using the internet.

How many times have you heard about someone in your industry, maybe even a direct competitor, who's experiencing wild success getting customers online?

I bet you've even clicked on their website to try and figure out what they are doing...only to start seeing their ads pop up in your Facebook feed and on almost every major website you visit.

It's as if they have a virtual spotlight following them around online, shining on them and trumpeting their expertise and positioning them as a leader in YOUR field. How have they achieved this celebrity-like status?

Their product or service may be no better than yours. It may even be worse; they just flat out don't come close to the quality you provide, and you know it! But it doesn't matter – because they're skyrocketing their success, and you're the one who's stuck. But you don't have to be.

Online marketing is extremely powerful, it's essential to keeping a steady stream of customers coming through the door, and it's here to stay.

As a business owner, you're used to wearing a lot of hats, and you may have been tempted to tackle it all on your own.

Maybe you've tried to run a Facebook ad or a Google Adwords™ campaign yourself. But despite your best efforts, online marketing hasn't come close to producing those kinds of results for your business.

It's not your fault. You already work WAY too hard and put in WAY too many hours just trying to create great products and services, tackle internal employee and production issues, as well as keep your customers happy. Struggling to keep up with the rapid changes in Google and Facebook on top of that can leave you burned out quickly! Don't worry; you're not alone.

I know it can be just as much of a struggle to find the right person or resources to make it work for you. You've probably been told by an online marketing consultant or agency that it's all a numbers game and that you just need more traffic. So you bit the bullet and hired them to do Search Engine Optimization (SEO), Pay-Per-Click Advertising (PPC), or maybe Social Media Marketing with the promise of getting you more traffic.

You sat back and waited, but nothing happened. Actually, you probably **did** get more traffic – maybe even a lot more traffic, just like they promised. But you didn't get the quality of leads and customers you thought that extra traffic would bring. So you're still stuck.

Unfortunately, a lot of business owners are experiencing the same thing, and I hear this all too often. After spending thousands, even tens of thousands, of dollars only to be left believing that online marketing success requires luck or being at the right place at the right time…or that it just won't work for their business, so they give up.

Don't.

Deep down you know internet marketing works. You've seen it working for others.

The question you're struggling to answer is "Why isn't it working for me?"

That's the same question I kept asking myself over and over again, just a few years ago.

I'd hit all the same brick walls you probably have, maybe more. I'd experienced the angst and despair of, "Is this ever going to work for me?" I spent thousands upon thousands of dollars of my own money with lackluster results. I was frustrated and stuck.

But I didn't stay that way.

Discovering the answer to one simple question, "Why isn't it working for me?" is why I do what I do today, and it's why I'm writing this book. I want to share what I have learned to save YOU the pain and heartache I went through trying to find the answer.

My Story

You see, just like you, I was good at my job. For me, that was up close and personal sales. I am talking about boots on the ground, in the trenches, pain-rich cold calling, door knocking sales! It didn't matter if it was a startup, a new company, or a Fortune 500 – everything I did turned to gold running through one brick wall after another (outworking the competition at every corner). As a 20-something serial entrepreneur and risk taker, I typically used the very scientific approach of jumping in, figuring it out on the fly, and just making it work!

With each new opportunity, my ego grew, and I also started to notice more and more the influence and leverage that digital marketing could create. At the time, the depth of my knowledge didn't go much beyond sending out mass emails. Yes, that's right; my philosophy at the time was everything was a "numbers game" in new lead generation, and I was going to SPAM the world to success!

Around this time, I was building a boutique oil and gas headhunting firm when virtually no one in the recruiting industry was embracing email automation or banner ad technology, and LinkedIn was just really starting to get going. Recruiting hadn't changed in 50 years; it is a business that requires a lot of organization and persistence to follow up with job candidates and hiring managers. So much business was lost because it was all being done by hand. I knew there was a better way.

I wanted to gain new clients online and communicate more effectively with candidates, and I did this by using the internet and automating my emails. I earned about $758,000 in new business in my first ten months.

I was hooked!

And with that success came bigger and bigger projects. With each new endeavor, there was a heavier reliance on technology. I started paying a lot more attention to online marketing. I realized not only that it played a huge part in the growth of established businesses, but also how startups were "growth hacking" their way to success in such a short time, mainly because of their online presence.

If you build it, they will come. Like most entrepreneurs, I thought it was all about getting more traffic to a website, but I quickly learned what it's really all about.

I knew online marketing worked. I saw how powerfully it was working for others. I even got a little taste of it myself with my email automation success.

So I went all in on my next endeavor. It was an aggressive undertaking that was almost entirely reliant on online lead generation.

I handed over $120,000+ to some internet marketing consultants to get my business desperately needed traffic. And like so many others, I waited with fingers crossed...

And nothing really happened.

It didn't even come close to achieving what I had expected it to achieve. We had failed.

Shocked, embarrassed, and disappointed, I wracked my brain for answers. It just didn't make sense. I knew internet marketing worked, so why didn't it work for me?

That question consumed me and started me on my journey to figure out WHY. WHY it didn't work for me, but more importantly, WHY it was working so successfully for a select few?

So I dove in. I joined a top internet marketing company to help me learn the "secret sauce."

That's when I discovered that I was missing one of the most critical pieces of the puzzle. I'm certain it is one of, if not the biggest, reason internet marketing hasn't been working for you either.

So what's the missing piece? **Transforming yourself into an authoritative brand that will attract your ideal customers.**

As you read this book and gain a deeper understanding of how to do this, together we will uncover the secrets that have led businesses in almost every industry to have unmatched success through online marketing and dominate their competition.

Many so-called online marketing experts promise, "Get to the first page of Google and your phone will ring off the hook," this is partly true, but we know better. That's not the whole story.

Yes, traffic is very important for getting your prospects to find you online. But what's truly important is giving them a reason to choose you over your competitors. Yet, this piece seems to be completely neglected by most businesses and even most online marketing consultants.

You see, when someone finds you on the front page of Google, they also find your competitors. It doesn't matter if you are a lawyer, dentist, remodeler, real estate agent, or pool and spa company. Your competitors are going after the same traffic you are.

Unfortunately, this competition is one of the main reasons businesses think they have to resort to competing on price. When you start going after customers who pick you because of price, you will get a customer who leaves you because of price. It is a race to the bottom, in my opinion.

But when you separate yourself from your competition with **value** (which is different from price) and go after customers who want to work with "the expert" in providing the solution they want, then positioning yourself as the authority or trusted adviser on the topic it gives them a stronger reason to pick you, **even if they have to pay more.**

Let me quickly differentiate between an "Expert" and an "Authority" before we move through the concepts and tactics in this book.

An Expert is someone who knows a lot about a particular subject. An Authority is not only knowledgeable but is also highly influential. If you can't communicate your knowledge, you will never be influential.

Get Started

Now that I have let you in on one of the biggest secrets of some of the most successful businesses in generating leads in every industry, you are at a critical fork in the road. Your actions now will influence where you are in a month, a year, and even 20 years from now. Are you happy with your current business or career trajectory? No? Then let's get started.

This book is a comprehensive guide on what to do and how to do it when it comes to increasing your presence, dominating your niche, and generating leads online. Throughout this book, I will share real-world tactics and examples that will help you build your authority and create "trusted advisor status" in your market. Not every business can utilize every single tactic, but rest assured that this book is packed full of great strategies you'll be able to put to work for YOUR company.

These tactics include:

- The science behind credibility – a factual basis to generate trust

- A blueprint to creating the reputation you want others to see online
- The hidden concepts behind affinity audiences, attraction marketing, and cause-based selling
- Case studies and real-world examples of people and businesses that achieved significant success through brand building
- A step-by-step explanation of how to build authority using the best tools, platforms, and resources online
- Why achieving a "Trusted Advisor Status," SERP stacking, and the celebrity effect are so important

Then, I will show you how to amplify and share your new status with far more prospects than you ever have before. I'll pull back the curtain on brand new ways you can use social media, paid ads, email automation and more...that no one else in your market is probably doing. This book is not hype, untested theory, or rehashed ideas on personal branding. These are tactics that I have personally helped implement for hundreds of clients and entrepreneurs.

The first step is to understand the actual science behind WHY this works so that you will be confident in the results you will achieve.

The Science of
Building Credibility

> *"The conscious mind determines the actions; the unconscious mind determines the reactions; and the reactions are just as important as the actions."*
>
> – *E. Stanley Jones*

People are often more willing to comply with a request or a recommendation when it comes from someone they perceive to be a legitimate "Expert" or "Authority." Think about the last suggestion you received from a doctor, therapist, or even your physical trainer. Did you feel compelled to take their advice? Why?

Throughout our lives, we are taught to follow and respect the accepted authorities within different hierarchical systems. This starts early on within the family unit, with a parent or grandparent, and then in school with a teacher or a principal, and continues in the workplace with a boss or supervisor.

We perceive someone as a legitimate authority when we assume that a person has earned or been given a high-ranking position, and therefore holds the right to exercise influence and command thought, opinion, or behavior within that realm (home, work, school, etc.). Once we have accepted the legitimacy of their authority, we adjust our mindset to comply.

This is an aspect of human nature gainfully exploited by con man Frank Abagnale (played by Leonardo Dicaprio in the movie *Catch Me If You Can*). In one of his legendary scams, Abagnale dresses up as a security guard and places a sign in front of a bank's night depository.

The sign reads, "NIGHT DEPOSITORY OUT OF ORDER — Please leave deposits with guard."

He then stands off to the side with a large cart, into which he places the money and receipts handed to him by trusting customers. At least 35 people drop bags or envelopes into his container. According to Abagnale, not one of them says more than "Good evening" or "Good night."

Since you might be skeptical of Frank Abagnale's story, here is a similar story that copywriter Dean Rieck loves to tell:

A television reporter dresses up in a security guard's uniform and sets up in front of a Las Vegas bank. He sticks a sign on the ATM embellished with a big gold badge and the following message:

"OUT OF ORDER — GIVE DEPOSITS TO GUARD ON DUTY."

Bank customers start showing up. Each time, the fake guard smiles and asks if the customer wants to make a deposit or withdrawal.

This whole scenario is ridiculous, right? No bank would conduct business this way.

And yet, customer after customer handed over cash, checks, Social Security numbers, credit cards, account numbers, PIN codes...you name it.

Out of 10 people, only one hesitated, but even he complied seconds later.

When the reporter revealed the deception and asked the flabbergasted victims why they handed him money and private information, they all gave pretty much the same answer:

"Because of the uniform. Because of the sign."

From these examples, we can see the influence that being viewed as an authority can bring. Our goal with branding should be to achieve authority status in the minds of our prospects and consumers in today's crazy world.

We must work hard to achieve this credibility through trust building but in a less nefarious way. Trust in your professional reputation is now more important than the quality of the products or services you sell according to the 2012 Edelman Trust Barometer (Edelman Trust Barometer, 2012), a survey on trust and credibility. I would argue it is now the most critical factor. Wary of scam artists, con men, rip-offs and shady marketing tactics, consumers are beginning to see the world in terms of "real" and "fake." Many have been burned, and now people base their purchasing decisions on how genuine they perceive an offer to be, how they feel about who is presenting the offer, and what customers have said through reviews.

Credibility is essential in all professions and at all times. This sense of authority calms jittery nerves and assures your clients that you are in control. Things sometimes don't go as planned if you are in a service-based business. Your clients and customers need to know they can trust you, and that you will do right by them. They need to know you also have the expertise and experience to get them through the troubled times as well as the good times. You need to be their safe harbor in the economic storm, the trusted guide that leads them through uncharted waters. However, if your credibility seems weak, your clients may get nervous when the boat rocks and take their business elsewhere.

This trustworthiness is essential to your success in many ways. It is your best weapon against fleeing customers and serves as a beacon to attract new ones. In almost every situation, CEOs and companies with solid credibility survive and thrive.

Credibility creates positive attitudes about you in your professional relationships, and who couldn't use more of that? Credibility is the barometer with which prospects, clients, competitors, and business partners judge you and, by extension, your business dealings. In fact, credibility drives your ability to raise capital, attract new clients, and negotiate great deals.

Establishing credibility does not always guarantee success or turn a prospect into a client, but it sure helps.

Building credibility can be challenging. Fortunately, there is a proven formula, which I attempt to distill for you as a business owner, entrepreneur, or salesperson who wants to position your company as the "go-to" brand. This formula will not only attract your ideal customers but also decrease the time needed to close a sale; it will also increase the lifetime value of each one of those customers!

It all starts with you. You have to build yourself as the trusted advisor. I will explain how to create solid connections with prospects as well as build credibility that will support your relationship as you nurture them into long-term clients.

The ancient Greek philosopher and scientist Aristotle was probably the first to think about scientifically building credibility. Aristotle created the "ingredients for persuasion" that, when mixed together in the right proportions, could persuade others to take a particular point of view. Otherwise known as "appeals," there were three main ingredients for persuasion:

1. Ethos: an appeal to ethics, used to convince someone of the credibility of the persuader
2. Pathos: an appeal to emotion, used to create a convincing emotional response
3. Logos: an appeal to logic and persuades the audience through reason

In other words, Aristotle believed that ethics were the first essential ingredient in convincing someone you are credible.

Medical researchers, psychologists, and sociologists can now support this and give us even greater insight into how the human mind works when it comes to decision making. Advanced technology, such as MRIs, helps scientists gain a better understanding of what happens in the brain while a person decides whether someone is trustworthy.

Let's delve into this a little deeper to build a solid foundation on where to start establishing ourselves as "Trusted Advisors".

Your prospects will judge you before you utter a word. Let me repeat that: *your prospects will judge you before you utter a word*, and your clients will continually reassess their opinions of you based on the way you act. This is based on Confirmation Bias which is the tendency to selectively search for and consider information that confirms one's beliefs.

When we meet someone, we tend to make a subconscious snap judgment based on how they look, act, or think, and then we look for evidence to support these judgments. We pay more attention to evidence that confirms our first impression than evidence that contradicts it.

Ever wonder why first impressions are so important? This is exactly why. You can improve your credibility by studying the way you appear to others upon meeting them. Credibility lives in the conscious and unconscious minds of both the individual trying to convey trustworthiness and in the person perceiving it. To build credibility, you must address the conscious and unconscious behaviors that build or erode trust. You must also understand the conscious and unconscious mind work together to assess credibility.

The unconscious mind works quietly in the background, evaluating information and making decisions. When you interact with others, you may exhibit unconscious behaviors that project details about your state of mind, competence, and credibility. Jingling change or keys in your pocket may make you seem nervous, for example. A prospect makes unconscious decisions about you when he or she sees you slouch, steeple your hands, or you tussle your hair. This is called Thin Slicing and is a shortcut that enables the brain to try to see the whole picture at once. Our unconscious finds patterns in behaviors or a situation based on very narrow slices of experience. We rapidly fill in incomplete images by drawing upon our prior experience.

For more information on building trust with conscious and unconscious behaviors, I recommend reading "How to Use Hand Gestures in a Powerful Way When You Communicate" in the "Social Triggers" blog by Derek Halpern.

7 Scientific Elements of Credibility

Credibility is built on a foundation of seven elements that are systematically arranged to maintain optimal strength and stability. As with the construction of a building, you must create each of the essential elements in the correct order.

1. Trust

Trust is essential in all types of economic and social transactions, from choosing a marriage partner to investing money. Establishing trust is critical for building credibility with your prospect – your client is, after all, entrusting you with their money/assets and time.

People who have suffered betrayal in the past will often avoid engaging in similar activities in the future. In other words, someone whose trust was broken by another will be slower to trust you. Watch out for this when meeting prospects.

Recent research (Margaret C. Wardle, 2013) shows the caudate, a small area near the center of your brain, decides whether you trust someone or not. The caudate becomes active when you deal with an unfair or indifferent person, but remains inactive when you deal with someone who is fair.

Additional research (Michael Kosfeld, 2005) shows that the hormone oxytocin plays a role in the formation of trust. It seems oxytocin shapes the circuitry (Oxytocin shapes the neural circuitry of trust and trust adaptation in humans. ,

2008) in three parts of the brain: the amygdala, the midbrain regions, and the dorsal striatum, which are also associated with trust.

You can foster a sense of trust with your prospects and clients by doing the following:

- Be on time. Show your prospect that you can be trusted with their most valuable resource: their time.
- Deliver on all your promises – large and small. Under-promise and over-deliver!
- Demonstrate a history of always doing what you say you're going to do. Provide examples of past successes.
- Show gratitude. A 2005 study (Schweitzer, 2005) by The Wharton School shows that anger decreases trust and gratitude increases it.
- Demonstrate they are in control in negotiations by using open-ended questions that start with "How" or "What," but never "Why."
- Consider closing your meetings by saying, "You decide. I trust your judgment." People are likely to reciprocate your trust in them with increased trust in you. Be polite and attentive. Remember that people often view polite and attentive individuals as being more trustworthy.

2. Communication

Maintaining open lines of communication helps build trust, confidence, and credibility. Your prospects need to feel that they can confide in you about their needs, dreams, resources, and apprehensions. They also need to believe that you will convey essential information to them quickly and accurately, and in ways they can understand.

The behavioral principle of Expressivity Halo suggests people also tend to feel more at ease with people who are easy to read or who communicate in an expressive fashion. This is because these people require less cognitive effort to decode.

Improve communication with prospects and clients by:

- Offering multiple means of communication, including email or texting
- Returning phone calls, texts, and emails quickly
- Using clear language
- Promptly following through on promises and projects
- Maintaining professional behavior, language, and dress
- Preparing for meetings and creating a meeting agenda so you can discuss all the major points without skipping important information
- Expressively talking
- Gesturing with your hands

3. Believability

Believability is defined as someone's confidence in the truthfulness of your claims without absolute proof. In other words, you must validate your prospect's first impression that you have their best interest in mind.

Your prospect won't be inclined to purchase from you unless they're confident they will receive the products or services expected. To ensure your customers will believe your products or services are as advertised:

- Provide specific data such as the number of years you've been in business, or the number of clients/customers served (Think McDonald's).
- Include testimonials and case studies on your website or marketing materials because they prove your product or service has been successful and this increases your believability.
- When discussing finances or statistics, providing specifics, such as percentages. Do not use vague terms such as "a lot of."
- Avoid exaggeration and hype, and tone down any claims that sound too good to be true.
- Provide a money-back guarantee whenever possible.

4. Relevancy

The Oxford English Dictionary defines relevancy as *the state of being closely connected or appropriate to the matter in hand.* To be relevant is to be important, but the term implies more than that; it means being the kind of person others depend on, whether for expertise, leadership, business sense, or social capital.

Relevancy helps give you the power to influence and alter events. To influence other people, you must talk about what they want or a problem they are trying to solve, then to show them how they can get what they want and give them the tools to solve the problem.

Some things you can do to increase your relevancy with your audience are:

1. Know what you are talking about – your audience expects you to provide detailed information

2. Help your clients and customers envision a positive outcome to their problem
3. Impress your clients by being thoughtful, careful, and creative
4. Associate with individuals or companies who believe in your product or services

5. Likeability

Likeability is a key predictor of success in all areas of life. From winning the bid for a big job or getting invited to the right parties to meet the right connections, likeability can get you where you want to go. Likeability pulls people toward you like an invisible magnet.

You can increase your likeability by:

- Having a genuine smile
- Making eye contact
- Maintaining a consistently positive mood
- Constantly engaging in personal self-improvement
- Leaving your judgments and opinions at the door
- Sharing the spotlight with others, especially your clients and prospects
- Being quick to apologize when you mess up

6. Safety

Making your clients feel safe is the foundation of credibility, especially when they are making a big decision or when their money might be at risk. You have to work hard to make them feel safe and turn off their fight-or-flight response.

When the fight-or-flight response is activated, nerve cells fire and chemicals like adrenaline, noradrenaline, and cortisol are released into the bloodstream. They become prepared, physically and psychologically, instinctively scanning the environment and looking for danger.

Seeing even a hint of someone expressing fear sparks a sense of fear in us as well. This is fundamentally how we engage in empathy. A mirror neuron fires both when we perform an action or when we see the same action performed by someone else.

Successful advisors are confident and "walk the walk" when it comes to demonstrating safety by:

- Exhibiting meticulous planning and forethought, and leading by example
- Being confident in yourself, your decisions, and your tone
- Providing prospects and clients with consistent feedback about the risks of a venture
- Demonstrating an ability to mitigate client risks
- Vocalizing a sense of responsibility for others' safety

7. Attractiveness

As superficial as it seems, trustworthiness also relies on appearance. Studies have shown that attractive people are perceived as more likeable and trustworthy. One study by Harvard University (Nancy L. Etcoff, 2011) indicates that we perceive attractive people as more likeable and trustworthy. Study participants viewed images of female faces with and without appearance-enhancing makeup and rated the faces according to attractiveness, competence, likeability, and trustworthiness. Faces wearing appearance-enhancing makeup were rated more trustworthy after just a quick glance (250 milliseconds) than were those without cosmetic enhancement.

I've noticed that pictures of good-looking people in Facebook ads produce much higher engagement and relevance scores than ads with people considered not as conventionally attractive. I have A/B tested many types of ads, and the results are consistent: attractiveness matters!

The amygdala is the part of your brain that judges other people's credibility by their faces – and it happens in just milliseconds. This is true even when you cannot clearly see faces. This means your clients make a snap judgment about you from only getting a glimpse of your face.

Don't worry; you don't have to be able to win a beauty contest or have washboard abs for success with this element. There are small ways you can spruce up your appearance enough to improve credibility. These steps might include:

- Take a good, hard look in the mirror to determine if your style is as appropriate, professional, and, most importantly, as attractive as possible
- Make sure your appearance is neat, fresh, with wrinkle-free clothing and styled hair
- Create a polished presentation: get organized, be on time, and prepare talking points
- Be polite and attentive
- Talk just enough: quiet people seem timid; loud people seem stubborn

Understanding the science behind building credibility can help you take your role as a trusted advisor up a notch. These seven elements are critical for building credibility within your market quickly. Incorporate these strategies into your business, and you will begin to stand out from the crowd.

So that's the basics. But you want more than the basics, right? Let's take it to the next level: now that your prospective customers consider you credible, it's time to start creating your reputation as a trusted advisor online.

Creating the Reputation You Want Others to See

It takes many good deeds to build a good reputation, and only one bad one to lose it.

– Benjamin Franklin

I feel like the internet has made everyone go bonkers. I thought technology was supposed to give us more time, but keeping up with Email, Facebook, LinkedIn, Blogs, Instagram, YouTube, Twitter, WordPress, and Google Analytics on a daily basis is dizzying! The internet has revolutionized the world in too many ways to count, but when it comes to your business or your personal goals, the main impact of the internet is its impact on your reputation.

Gone are the days when the things you do in your private life are separate from your professional life. With the internet today, all it takes is one post to completely change your reputation, either for the better or for the worse.

This is why online reputation management, or ORM, is something you need to take very seriously.

ORM involves careful strategies to ensure that what is being said about you online is both accurate and positive while maintaining your professional and personal brand in your interactions with people online.

However, reputation *management* is just one side of the coin in building a solid online reputation; reputation *manufacturing* is the other. Creating a solid online reputation requires both.

What Is Reputation Management?

The Business Dictionary defines Reputation Management as "activities performed by an individual or organization which attempt to maintain or create a certain frame of mind regarding themselves in the public eye."

Reputation management may involve:

- Identifying what others are saying or feeling about a business
- Taking steps to ensure that those opinions are in line with the business's goals
- Using social media to monitor the company's reputation

How does this look in a real-life situation?

Reputation management refers to shaping public perception of yourself or your organization by attempting to influence the information about you or your company that is posted online.

This involves a number of tactics, including:

- Adding authority-building content
- Being aware of mentions people make about you online

- Reacting to those mentions appropriately
- Addressing any content that could potentially damage your reputation
- Actively engaging with customer feedback
- Solving problems before people post anything hurtful to your image

Now take a moment to consider if someone was to scroll through your Facebook newsfeed right now. What would it say about you? What snapshot do your posts and images portray to your prospects, customers, and future employees?

Reputation - who cares about that anyway?

Everyone should.

For business owners, entrepreneurs, and professionals, it all comes down to the lifeblood of any business: sales and customers.

In most cases, the final step a prospect will take before deciding between you or other vendors is a Google Search. They will search for your name to look for information to help them make their decision. You want to make sure they only see things that persuade them to choose you; more confirmation bias is needed.

Many people don't think their online reputation is at risk. Perhaps they avoid social media or use it only for the most professional of posts. Maybe they think that they do not have a website, so therefore no one is talking about them online. Since they don't post incriminating evidence on their own, they feel they are safe.

Newsflash: They're wrong.

Users can tag you on Facebook without your consent, post online reviews about your business even if you don't have a website, and they can talk about you many places across the internet that will show up in Google searches without your knowledge.

Your reputation is far more fragile than you would believe and can be damaged quickly and easily.

According to a new survey conducted by Dimensional Research, an overwhelming 90% of respondents who recalled reading online reviews claimed that positive online reviews influenced their buying decisions, while 86% said their buying decisions were influenced by negative online reviews (Dimensional Research, 2013).

Just one disgruntled former employee or a heartbroken old flame can cause severe damage to your reputation online.

I say this from personal experience. If those angry individuals decide to air your dirty laundry online, your digital reputation will take a serious hit. Someone who wants to damage your personal or professional reputation can be quite successful with just a few keystrokes. That's the power of the internet today.

Reputation Management Case Study

Consider, as an example, the epic meltdown that occurred on the Amy's Baking Company Bakery Boutique & Bistro Facebook page a few years back. This Scottsdale, AZ restaurant was featured on *Gordon Ramsey's Kitchen Nightmares*.

Unfortunately, this episode brought some bad publicity to the restaurant, and when those who saw the episode started chiming in on Facebook with negative reviews and comments, the owners took the defensive, turning the criticism into an online battle of epic proportions.

The entire thing went viral, further damaging the reputation of the restaurant. Negative comments about the restaurateurs started appearing on Reddit, Yelp, and Facebook, and the husband-and-wife team allegedly began posting torrents of abuse directed back at the commenters.

One message, presumably from husband Samy, read:

"To all of the Yelpers and Reddits: Bring it on. you are just p***. come to Arizona. you are weaker than my wife, and weaker than me. come to my business. say it to my face. man to man. my wife is a jewel in the desert. you are just trash, reddits and yelpers just working together to bring us down. pathetic."

If the business had made changes after the TV episode and responded to the first few negative reviews with an explanation of what they learned from the experience and how they changed their business, they may have been able to salvage their reputation.

Instead, they got defensive and engaged in heated arguments with their critics, which ended up hurting them more.

I was told from a young age, "Don't do anything that you would mind having as a front-page story in the newspaper the next morning."

This rings truer than ever today with the virality of social platforms like Twitter! #GoldenRule

With reputation management in place, the restaurant's owners would have had a plan to implement when negative reviews surfaced, giving them a strategy to employ before this meltdown erupted.

That incident shows how quickly one negative post or comment can derail a business and ruin its good name. If someone has a desire to do you harm, it just takes a moment for irreparable damage to be done.

Hence, you must be ready to properly address any negativity you find online to protect your reputation.

The same is true for your business. Potential customers and clients are going online to see what past customers and clients say about you before they hire you. They not only want to see positive reviews but also that you are knowledgeable about your craft.

If you are a medical professional, and the only reviews people find about your practice are negative reviews from unhappy patients (even those impossible-to-please ones who won't be happy no matter what you do), you are going to struggle to grow your practice. Doctors and Administrators should be addressing this; people are reading these reviews. I see this way too often!

Consider another situation where maybe a doctor uses their name as the business name. What happens when a potential client searches for the doctor's name and finds a person with a criminal record by the same name?

While the doctor may be an expert in their field, their perceived reputation may be overshadowed, and they might lose new clients because of it.

Are you using your name for your business? What comes up online when people search for you? You must consider the internet real estate that could be associated with you or your business.

No matter what field you are in, from food service to financial planning, your online presence needs to reflect your industry and your competency properly, and reputation management is a key component. **If you don't know what is being said about you, what people are finding when they search for you, or you cannot be found online, your business will suffer.**

Many of us started using Facebook, Twitter, and Instagram when they were just a fun way to share pictures of a vacation or a new baby. What you were posting five years ago, however, is not the same as what you should post today.

You already know that, though. What you *don't* know is that those posts are still around, and could be found by an employer or prospect who won't be understanding of the fact that you've matured. We all mature (well, most of us anyway), and part of that maturation process involves making sure there aren't any embarrassing pictures of us online.

A strong element of brand building is *un*-building the statements you may have made about yourself in previous years. Make sure to:

- Remove photos that contain alcohol, cigarettes, inappropriate clothing, or public displays of affection.
- Use clean, professional pictures that include only the bust up on all your profiles. The exception to this rule is freelancers and entrepreneurs using a logo instead.
- Remove grumpy status updates.
- *Especially* remove any negative references to former bosses.

Don't just deal with the known offenders; Google yourself and carefully track down all posts that might prove offensive to a future client or employer. If you don't think you can do it yourself, try using a reputation management app, you can hire a reputation management service (but this is admittedly an extreme measure).

Online Reputation Management

Online reputation management involves three components.

1. Curtailing the negative things that others are publishing about you online.
2. Highlighting your personal brand to ensure you are seen as an expert in the field for which you wish to find success.
3. Ensuring clients can easily find you. You might be the best in a particular field, but if no one knows how good you are or worse, who you are, it's all for naught.

You must gain the visibility and influence to even be an option for a potential prospect who is making a buying decision. By doing these things consistently, you will be able to ensure your online reputation is a positive one and your business will thrive.

That is just the starting point. Learning to manage your online reputation is essential, but once you have a good handle on reputation management, you need to start working on *Reputation Manufacturing.*

What Is Reputation Manufacturing?

"If you don't like what is being said, then change the conversation."

— *Don Draper, Mad Men*

The final step a prospect will take before deciding between vendors often comes down to a Google search.

You not only want to prevent negative results from showing up that will damage your chances of being selected by a prospect, but you also want to make sure authority-building pieces show up in the search results. This is the basis of Reputation Manufacturing.

Reputation Manufacturing involves creating good things for other people to say about you online, things that you probably can't say about yourself.

This can be achieved through published articles you wrote for authority sites, being interviewed by the media, press releases, or simply from reviews and testimonials posted by satisfied clients.

By highlighting these things online, you can shape your reputation and build your brand. This works hand in hand with reputation management to solidify your brand and improve the positive image others have of you.

How Reputation Manufacturing Works

Reputation Manufacturing involves two key strategies:

1. Have positive items written about yourself or your business. Once they are out there, you ensure that

proper SEM and SEO helps them fill up the search and social results. Why is this important? Because having *other people* write good things about you helps solidify your reputation. If you wrote good things about yourself, it would only be self-serving. By having others post good reviews and comments, that is taken out of the equation.

2. Add enough positive items to ensure those items are what people see first when they search for your name.

With Reputation Manufacturing, you can "get ahead" of your reputation management, working proactively instead of reactively. Below are some techniques you can use to help manufacture your reputation.

Start With Google

Google has become synonymous with the internet due to its overweight marketing share of all online search results. Keep this in mind as you build your brand.

Before doing anything else, set up a Google alert for your name, nickname, and company name at Google.com/alerts. Include all versions of your name, even common misspellings, to ensure you have all your bases covered. This way, you are notified any time someone posts about you or your company.

When you receive an alert, make sure the item posted is consistent with the goals for your brand, and if it is not, take action.

If you have already set up Google alerts and need more advanced options, you can set up alerts with a free Hootsuite account or use paid services like Radian6, but Google is by far the easiest.

Next, Google your name and your business name. See what comes up in the top 5–10 results. If you're not happy with what you see, create some new posts to get your positive information pushed to the top.

I currently have a client that is very high up in the network marketing industry. An unhappy past consultant took action against him, and negative information was appearing on the first page of the search results.

That one disgruntled person's actions started to overshadow my client's other accolades. He took one company from zero to $125,000,000 and then another to $400,000,000. His success and ability were no coincidence, but one person had the power to taint all that.

After getting to know him, I learned that he was a good guy with a wonderful story to share. Together we came up with a strategy to promote his business and clean up his online reputation.

We created highly relevant, authority-building content, pushing him higher up in Google search results and outranking the negative results.

Through this strategy, we were able to push the negative results to the second page of Google and fill up the first-page search results with information that helped us better tell his story to new prospects in a positive way.

A quick joke: Where is the best place to hide something you don't want someone to find?

The second page of Google!

Sorry; lame industry joke, but I couldn't help myself.

Learn the Art of SERP Stacking

SERP refers to the Search Engine Results Page. SERP stacking involves claiming as much real estate across all platforms as possible and placing a sign in that real estate with the information you want others to see about you or your company.

While this is not by any means an exhaustive list of SEO strategies, this is more about making sure you have a good foundation of completed profiles indexed at all the major Web 2.0 social and review sites around the internet.

The more sites (beyond your personal or business website) that use your name and your information, the better your reputation will be. Your site will also gain Domain Authority by creating an additional "backlink" to your site.

There are several proven strategies I will touch on in this chapter that you can employ to get that information out there and manufacture a positive image of yourself and your company online, but I recommend starting with directories and business listings.

Become an Online Real Estate Tycoon

Have you considered that your website and blog are the only pieces of online real estate that you own? Everything else is rented property that you could lose, or the rules could be changed on you at any time.

I am a huge proponent of controlling as best you can and as much as you can of your online real estate.

If you don't have a website for your company or yourself, invest today. It is worth it.

In addition to your company domain, purchase the domain for your name. Also, create continuity with your social media profiles. If your name is unavailable, consider adding your niche before or after your name.

Many people in the SEO space will write "SEO" after their name. For example, www.MattBertramSEO.com. Doing this is beneficial because not only does it give Google a better idea of what you do, but it also helps you find unclaimed profiles so that you can create brand consistency. Consider a tool like knowem.com to help you find and register hundreds of unclaimed profiles quickly.

Now, let's take a step back. Before you go claiming all this digital land, we need to make sure your "money site" is optimized.

All your business listings should point back to an online property you own, like your business or personal website.

Let's make sure the house is in order before we invite guests. Are your website technicals and on-page SEO correct? Like your car, a website needs a checkup now and then. Here's how to take a look under the hood:

- Ensure structured data and tags (Schema markup) are filled out and labeled properly for Google to understand your website
- Check for duplicate content
- Optimize images for load time and make sure it's mobile friendly
- Make sure the SSL Certificates are setup properly
- Resolve any 404 errors and fix any bad links

Google hates bad links or "roads to nowhere." They want only to show sites that provide a good experience for the user. Make sure that the site structure makes sense, your pages flow logically, and there is easy navigation for your visitors.

You should treat your website as your main lead-generating tool and not just a digital brochure. The internet has evolved and so how you use your website must evolve as well.

There is quite a lot to cover on this topic, and I will touch on some of these best practices later when talking about landing pages, but I would also recommend either *Landing Page Optimization* by Tim Ash or *Website Optimization: An Hour a Day* by Rich Page for more on website optimization.

If you have an older website, it would also be wise to get an audit. You don't know what might be hurting you. Fixing any errors helps your website skyrocket to the top of the search results. Visit BuildYourBrandMania.com/Resources to access free tool to do a quick website scan and see how you rank.

About Me

Create a quality "About Me" page – not just on your website but also on multiple platforms. The "About Me" section is the best place to tell your story and sell yourself, your expertise, and your company. Many business owners often overlook this section.

1. Put your name and title right up front in the title tags. Don't make your prospects work hard to find your full name and exactly what you do.

2. Invest in a quality, professional headshot. Prospective customers want to see with whom they might be working. Help your visitor connect with you long before they pick up the phone for that initial consultation. Using an unprofessional image, like cropping your head out of a family photo at the beach, can hurt you more than not having a profile image. Also, make sure to use the same headshot across all platforms. Consider even a video introduction.

3. Provide a summary of what you do for your clients. Walk your prospects through your process. Tell them what it's like to meet with you. Explain what you will do to help them with their specific problem. The more specific you can get here, the better. Tell the story of why you do what you do. I've dedicated a full chapter in this book to storytelling. Use the concepts in that chapter to help tell your story on your About Me page.

4. List highlights of relevant accomplishments, awards, and media appearances.

5. Include some personal information. You are so much more than what you do. Prospective clients like to know some personal details because it helps them relate to you. The more they can relate, the easier it is to build trust with them. Tell them what you do in your free time, or the fun activities you partake in with your family. A small snapshot of who you are as a person can go a long way to help build a strong relationship.

6. Always provide your direct contact information. List your direct phone line, an email address, and your business address so prospects can reach you. Offer a downloadable Virtual Contact File (vCard), if possible. Post links to relevant social media profiles where you are most active, such as Facebook, LinkedIn, or Twitter.

Have You Heard? Social Is the New SEO!

You want people to hear about you. Well, the "About Me" does not only refer to your website these days. Have you heard of About.me?

When building a brand, you should complete as many profiles as you can on different social channels. Make sure you keep it consistent. Again use the same headshot and title across all platforms. In addition to your About.me and other platforms, be sure to create a Gravatar (Globally Recognized Avatar) to target your name and link them all together. These act as Social Citations and help let Google know you are a brand, similar to directory building with NAP (Name Address Phone) listings in Local SEO. Claiming this online real estate will build backlinks and SERP ranks.

Social platforms have become more and more like search engines, using hashtags and the search bar to find topics and information in which users are interested.

Broadcast Yourself

Make sure to maximize your Google properties, including YouTube. YouTube isn't just quickly becoming one of the largest search engines in the world – it already is! Three hundred hours of video are uploaded to YouTube every minute, and almost five billion videos are watched on YouTube every single day! YouTube videos have descriptions and titles that can rank in Google searches. Also, Google owns YouTube, so they give it preferential treatment (This goes for Google+ and Google My Business, properties as well).

Establishing a YouTube channel should be a staple for your personal or business branding goals. Fill it with relevant video content complete with optimized descriptions and links to your website to help improve your search engine results. Post blog content to Google Plus for terms you want to rank for.

Facebook is the New Home Page

"Think about what people are doing on Facebook today. They're keeping up with their friends and family, but they're also building an image and identity for themselves, which in a sense is their brand. They're connecting with the audience that they want to connect to. It's almost a disadvantage if you're not on it now."

– Mark Zuckerberg

Many people start their day on Facebook and end their day on Facebook. To be found, you need to be where the people are. Business pages on Facebook often rank first or second on Google. They sometimes rank above a company's optimized site due to Facebook's strong trust and domain authority rankings, which are critical for businesses in competitive markets, so your profile needs to be as complete as possible. Then, start building followers by posting relevant content that solves the problems of your target market.

Instagram

Instagram is a fantastic visual platform that is here to stay and offers users an excellent way to increase their digital footprint. Instagram gives you a creative way to tell your company's story using photos, video, and gifs. You can frequently add or edit information to your Instagram bio. Keep your audience interested with teaser photos to build anticipation in your product releases and make your followers feel special by allowing them to preview upcoming events.

Twitter is a Conversation

Twitter is the most public form of communication among people and brands online today. 1,300,000,000 people use Twitter, and it is widely used for PR and connecting with market influencers. The Brand Pages that are very similar to Facebook give companies a more distinctive presence while providing another strong SERP citation.

I often get asked about Twitter, specifically how to use it as well as questions about bots. Think of Twitter as your company's voice. Imagine yourself in a public park walking around with all the people you want to hang out with or would ever want to meet. Just start getting to know them. Follow people, thank them for following you. Like posts, re-tweet posts. Direct message people. If you post something of interest to others, use a hashtag like #itshowpeoplefindstuff. Link it to your Facebook. Think of Twitter as the real-time you, online. Bots are prevalent, but there are still a ton of real people.

Twitter is an up-to-the-minute, 24/7 platform, which is why it's become such an effective platform for news. Try cross-posting things you find interesting or useful on Twitter to Facebook. Many people use Facebook to find news. Twitter news spreads like wildfire and chances are people that follow you on Facebook might not have seen it yet. (This also creates another backlink from one social property to another and strengthens your overall relevancy through your network!) Make a Twitter list, and follow people who might be relevant to the audience that you are targeting to pick up some creative content to share or retweet. Give people a reason to follow you!

Become an Expert on LinkedIn

LinkedIn is one of the best places to help stack your SERPs and create positive social signals for your website. First, you need to set up a company page where you can publish articles, create a tagline, have personal and business page profiles, and receive recommendations or endorsements from people who have done business with you. You can also give recommendations, and like, share, and comment on content to help brand yourself as an expert in your niche. LinkedIn lets you create and distribute content and blogs to build your authority. LinkedIn also recently bought Slideshare adding to the strength of their distribution channel. If you aren't on LinkedIn, you need to be.

Get Discovered on Pinterest

Pinterest is an online shareable pinboard of images, quotes, and just plain cool ideas! The platform recently added a social component where others can see and interact with various boards and pins that people create. You can like, comment, and re-pin each other's stuff easily now.

I think this is going to be the best platform for advertisers and promoters in the future. Set up a business profile today, and you will be ahead of the curve. Some companies have entire SEO strategies based on the rankings they get from Pinterest.

Become Internet Famous Through Podcasting

Consider starting a podcast or be a guest on multiple podcasts. If you can get others to interview you about your subject of expertise, it can definitely help your search engine results. These mentions are very powerful. Why? Because the title of the podcast and the description will usually have your name and your industry in the search results. Also, if you receive a backlink, it will be hard for your competitors to replicate this unique mention. For example, I am the Co-Host of an eight-year-long podcast called *"The Unknown Secrets of Internet Marketing" SEO Podcast*. The title uses two keywords, SEO and Internet Marketing, which are associated with what I do, to help me rank highly for those keywords.

Doing interviews will help brand you as an authority in your industry, because after all, someone thought you were knowledgeable enough to interview you, right? Not to mention you will get exposure to their audience, which is a huge plus. Podcast booking services such as *Interview Connections* or *Be My Guest* are available, but doing some basic outreach is not hard; if you have an assistant, they can probably do it for you. If you decide to start a podcast, check out sites like Podomatic or Stitcher – they make it simple.

Contribute to BuzzFeed

Feel like no one will interview you yet? Well, I have some good news. Just about anyone can contribute content to *BuzzFeed*, and it's one of the most highly trafficked sites in the world. *BuzzFeed* articles themselves do not have an SEO benefit because Google blocks these, but your author page will appear in the SERPs when people search for you, and you will start to brand yourself as an expert. The same thing goes for forums like Quora. I love helping people out and answering questions on Quora. I currently get about 4750+ views a week on my posts.

Be Active With Guest Posting

Guest posting is one of the easiest and most effective ways to take up real estate in the SERPs. Posting as a guest blogger on high-ranking third party websites that provide the option for an "About the Author" bio and link will spread your reach to your target customers while increasing your rank in the search engines. Also, having these links connected to your guest posting will provide off-page SEO benefits for your website. It pays dividends to be active in the online communities and forums.

As you can see, building a solid reputation online takes work, but I promise you the dedication is worthwhile. With a little effort and planning, and an emphasis on reputation manufacturing, you can ensure that the things people see and hear about you are in line with your personal and business branding goals.

Now that you have made it easy for prospects to find you online by cleaning up your existing online reputation and creating more positive search engine results, you are ready to take the next step.

I will show you how to ensure that once a prospect finds you online, they will never, ever forget you.

How to Create a Personal Brand

The sooner you create your personal brand, the better. The longer you go without branding yourself, the more time your competition has to establish a relationship with your prospects. Branding is not just about being seen as a better option than your competition; it's about being seen as the *only* solution to your prospect's problem.

Branding isn't about market share; it's about mindshare, and it works in any market, big or small. Brands have to do less selling. They have a relationship with their target market and have a high level of trust. A strong brand has people chasing them vs. the other way around. Branding is about emotion, and emotion turns prospects into buyers. People connect with people, not a product or a faceless company.

How does this translate to positioning online? I remember one of the things that a nationally top-ranked SEO consultant told me the day we met: "Google loves brands. Creating brand lift is one of the fastest ways to shoot up to the top of the rankings."

Dr. Milad Shadrooh came to mind and is a perfect example of someone who not only has created brand lift, but also has improved his credibility, status, and practice by building a personal brand. Being aware of the pitfalls associated with his career (i.e., a dentist on every corner) he decided to build a brand. He became "The Singing Dentist" and promoted oral health by making dentistry fun through parody and song, and has become a rock star of sorts. He also builds on this status by hosting community fundraisers, and he participates in local charity events to further gain exposure for his brand in the local area as well as give back.

The Singing Dentist now enjoys tremendous success, with more than 419,388 followers on Facebook and a YouTube channel with more than 86,000 followers. He is for sure the "go-to" dentist for anyone with kids living near his practice. Dentistry.co.uk even named Milad Shadrooh as the most influential dentist of 2017!

The Importance of Branding Yourself

If you own a small business, then you already know the importance of branding. Chances are you've spent some time trying to figure out how you can market your business to make it stand out from the rest. Branding is a concept that's not new to you. However, I'm willing to bet that, for all the effort you've exerted on branding your business, you've probably not spent much time, if any at all, branding YOURSELF to your target audience.

Depending on your goals and aspirations, that is probably a huge mistake.

For someone who is content to struggle, barely cover their expenses, and wants to stay out of the public eye, a personal brand might not be that important. But for everyone else – those of you who are looking to make a mark in this world – then a personal brand is imperative!

Regardless of what business you're in, taking the time to think about how best to market yourself as a person, rather than just your business, is essential and can pay dividends long into the future.

Need more convincing?

First, even though you are putting your heart and soul into your business, you should not have your identity wholly tied to it. Companies come and go. At some point, you might decide you're ready to sell, or close down, or keep it going but start something new. At that point, your future is more tied to your name than your business. Think Donald Trump – need I say more?

Also, your personal brand can help your existing business. A recognizable name brings people in. If your name is known and trusted, people will seek you out, your name drawing them to your business and services.

Finally, branding is all about preparation. There is no telling what is going to happen weeks, months, or even years down the road. Don't wait until you need a personal brand to start thinking about it because by then it will be too late. The more you think about and work on your brand now, the more prepared you are for the future, no matter what happens.

How to Get Started

Many keys come into play when you're trying to build a brand, but one of the most important is that you always provide something of value. After all, that's what an Authority or a Trusted Advisor does: gives good advice.

In every industry, people are looking for experts. While you may charge for this advice sometimes – such as consulting, or when doing a workshop – you must also give it away for free sometimes.

Notice I didn't say, "You *can* give it away for free." I said "*must*," and that's intentional. I would even say give your best stuff away for free, too, but that might be too much for you to process right now. Just know, it works. People will be lining up if you prove that **you can help them.**

If prospects visit your website and see nothing but options to buy, they won't have an incentive to keep reading, and they will have no proof that you're the expert who can solve their problem. You need to either demonstrate to them that you are an expert, or they need to hear a third party call you an authority, or read something to determine you are indeed an expert.

I achieve this through testimonials, case studies, webinars, our weekly podcast, writing this book, and doing guest interviews or speaking engagements. Our company does something we call a "deep dive," or "profit plan," which is a one- to two-hour strategy session with a money-back guarantee. (To date, the one time a client asked for a refund they later came back to spend twice as much!) We demonstrate our expertise and prove our value first-hand. I think it's important to understand that typically the person who delivers the most value wins.

So what should you be doing to step into the role of "a Trusted Advisor" for your prospects and customers?

Educate, Educate, Educate

"You will get all you want in life, if you help enough other people get what they want."

– Zig Ziglar

Information is the new form of online currency. Strive to give away great information.

I recently heard a great nugget of wisdom at a conference in San Diego. We were discussing how to use different types of offers and lead captures. The key is to give away something for which someone would gladly pay. Educating means giving them the tools they need to see results, or even just answering their questions. People come to experts because they believe those experts can help them, and consistently posting educational content does just that.

Instead of trying to prove your expertise with complicated, drawn-out explanations or outright claims of your greatness, **show them.** People want to hear about past success from others, and they want to see it work with their own eyes. Everyone is skeptical these days. Many have been burned before. It's not you; it's them! They will have their guard up. Providing value up front will give you access to the reciprocity shortcut in the human behavior decision-making process. In other words, offering them value leads to them reciprocating in some way, maybe with a review, referral, or possibly buying from you.

For more details on the benefits of reciprocity, as well as five Principles of Influence (Scarcity, Authority, Consistency, Liking, and Consensus), read *Influence: The Psychology of*

Persuasion by Robert B. Cialdini. Utilizing these principles will help your business gain a competitive edge. When writing direct response copy for clients, I employ these concepts and find that typically the more principles I use, the more compelling the copy becomes and the more conversions I see.

For example, financial expert Dave Ramsey uses reciprocity. He posts various tips and articles on his website for his customers free of charge and takes advantage of the law of reciprocity.

He also offers seminars that help his customers learn more about money management and even provides free printable resources. All these elements are examples of how Dave Ramsey educates his audience of prospective and current clients.

The best-known and most successful companies in every industry offer advice on *how to* accomplish a specific goal that the prospect is looking to achieve: how to lose weight in actionable steps, how to select the right cabinets for a kitchen remodel, or how to get out of a DWI.

However, the main point I want you to focus on is *one* problem your ideal customers are looking to solve and solve it. Just one. You can, of course, offer many solutions to many different problems, but target each piece of consumable content and make sure it is easy to apply to the current issue. Don't discount the importance of this; offering too much information at once might confuse them, and your prospects will head to an expert who can offer more straightforward advice.

Our brain chemistry is also a contributing factor in this behavior. Dopamine is a neurotransmitter that helps control the brain's reward and pleasure pathways. It's one of our body's triggers for motivation and what keeps us going. Prospects want a quick win which gives them a quick shot of dopamine. I firmly believe this is why people love checklists and guides so much.

Once you begin building your brand as "A Trusted Authority," it becomes easier to reach more people, educate larger crowds, and continue building trust. Then you can expand your reach into different areas. It's a virtuous circle with the serious benefit of improving lives along the way.

Advocate for Your People

Advocating is related to educating, with the critical difference that you are also taking action in favor of your customers and prospects. Now you're not only giving them the tools to succeed, but you're also helping people use them effectively.

Merely talking about how something works isn't enough, showing people they should trust and work with you is another thing. They need you to hold their hands, answer their questions, and connect with them as a true advocate.

Advocates respond personally to email. They offer free training and live calls to help customers employ new technology, concepts, or products. They give their time to people who need answers.

Don't think you can't provide value. On our podcast, Chris Burres and I share input on articles that we have first-hand knowledge of from SEO and PPC campaigns we are running. We are just curating the content. You can do this too, and with anything. We are all experts at something.

You may wonder if this is a valuable use of your time once a week. Well, our audience has grown to about 26,000+ listeners globally, and on average, between the podcast and referrals, they provide about 65% of our business. We don't ever have to hunt for business, so I can focus on what I do best, as well as what I love to do most: helping people with their online marketing!

The business is watered, fertilized, and gradually grows each week. When it is ripe, they call us. Only about 3% of prospects are immediately ready to buy when you talk to them. Instead of cold calling like I used to do (50-80 calls a day) to find a needle in a haystack, why not attract them to you like moths to a flame? When podcast listeners call, they are already pre-sold; we just have to explain how the process works, determine their needs, and where to sign. Positioning yourself as "A Trusted Authority" is the best thing you can do for your business and yourself. It's a much better way to do business in the "new economy."

How are you going to be spending your time for the next six months? Consistently make an effort to educate and advocate for the people who need you. (Go to the platforms where your prospects already are: Facebook, LinkedIn, Quora, iTunes, etc.) They will trust that you have their best interests at heart, and will also refer people to you, all because of a simple mindset shift on how you think about and position yourself and your business to them.

You are an authority on something. Make that shift to create one of the most memorable brands in your industry today!

Support a Cause You Believe In

The law of attraction states that "like attracts like." Science has shown that people tend only to form relationships with people who hold the same values, views, and prejudices.

Ethan Zuckerman is a technologist and blogger that has some great Ted Talks discussing how the world is connected as well as the impact of the internet. He shares a story about a marketer I follow, Seth Godin, who wants to change the world. He also believes Seth has a formula that allows people to make big, disproportionate changes by bringing groups of people together. It's fascinating!

Godin tells the story of Nathan Winograd, who was an executive at the San Francisco SPCA. Winograd believed the organization's mission shouldn't be the killing of dogs and cats. Did you know that each year, four million dogs and cats are killed, most within 24 hours of reaching a shelter? Winograd advocated that San Francisco become a no-kill city. To fight the enormous pushback, he had to develop grassroots support to overturn the laws in not just San Francisco, but also in Tompkins County, New York; Reno, Nevada; and in North Carolina! I am a huge animal lover, and this story touched me; it's refreshing to know that one person can start a movement to change the world.

It's a mistake to believe that you can simply put together a cause, then wait for the masses to recognize its genius and come running to join. There are a lot of other things going on under the surface.

People crave community, and the community's purpose needs to speak to them on a significant level. They also need to know that they can make a difference with measurable goals. Most causes, after all, have their figurative hearts in the right place. But with a world so desperately in need, we could all donate thousands of dollars a day and not see a difference. That is why the Save the Children infomercials focus mainly on one or two kids. People feel they can make an impact and save one child versus a drop in the bucket towards this monumental problem.

When starting a movement, Seth Godin advises you to ask yourself three questions:

1. Who are you upsetting? If you're not upsetting anyone, you're not changing the status quo.
2. Who are you connecting?
3. Who are you leading?

Make it clear to your prospective community what they'll be a part of and what your higher theme is. Equality? Hope? Health?

Michelle Obama's *Let's Move* campaign succeeds because it's tied so intricately to the health of our youth, something we value. What are *you* offering that plays on the public heartstrings, that sticks in people's heads and won't let go? Make it easy for them to connect with you and share the message through social media. Have milestones and celebrate them.

Do Something Meaningful

Giving to a cause is all well and good, but too often follows the same model: A foundation issues a heartfelt plea, you send in money, and the money disappears into the void. Sometimes a thank you follows, sometimes not. People are exhausted by this model, no matter how well-intentioned it might be.

That's why people embrace Kickstarter. This now-beloved platform enables people to do something truly meaningful, and then see the results of their contribution. Instead of just ferreting away money and hopefully doing something real with it, Kickstarter campaigns lay out very, very clearly what will happen with the money they receive, and offer gifts at tiered donation levels. You donate this amount; you get a sticker. At this higher donation level, you get a t-shirt or even the ability to buy the product before it's released.

Then you could run a contest on social media and ask people that supported the campaign to take pictures using the product, showing the stickers, or wearing the shirts. This is a great way to create User Generated Content (UGC) and build more exposure for your brand without you or your team doing all the work. Take a note from these massive social media platforms that have it figured out.

WIIFM (What's in it for Me)

It's not likely that people are supporting your cause just for fun. People will join you in your nascent movement, helping you turn it into a real, full-blown cause if they sense that they'll get something out of it. We're not just talking about money or even recognition; perhaps all they want is personal fulfillment or the comforting feeling of battling the disease responsible for the death of a family member.

"What's in it for me?" doesn't necessarily have to be directly related to the cause either, but should be considered.

Lots of people race for the cure because they care about keeping themselves in shape just as much as they care about cancer awareness. By signing up for a run, they pit themselves against a deadline. The fact that they can raise money for a great cause is even better, but not always the chief motivator.

You want others to know you are involved in the community and that you give back. That's why we include our logos on pink shirts and ribbons for Breast Cancer Awareness Month or the wildly growing Love Your Melon hats to support childhood cancer research.

Apparel isn't the only way to do this, though. The iconic Ice Bucket Challenge is dedicated to raising awareness for amyotrophic lateral sclerosis, otherwise known as ALS, or motor neuron disease. The challenge shows people dumping buckets of ice water over their heads and videotaping the results, then nominating others to do the same. Those who don't want to can choose to donate to ALS fundraising efforts instead.

Want your cause to stand for something? Give your followers a way to make themselves stand out. A hashtag. A bracelet. A catchphrase. A website badge. No matter what it is, make sure it is visually inspiring as well as truly meaningful, and people will line up behind it.

Creating a cause you believe in is more than a great way to help a world that needs help in more ways than we can count; it's also a powerful way to garner attention for your business' products and services and generate a ton of great content doing it. So next time you're scratching your head, wondering how to create that brand you crave, ask yourself: What's your cause? Then bring it to the world as only you can.

How to Develop a Brand That's Right for You

Recently, Facebook COO Sheryl Sandberg of *Lean In* fame declared personal brands a myth: "You don't have a brand. Crest has a brand. Perrier has a brand. You don't have a brand, but you do have a voice."

People are not that simple. We're not packaged. And when we are approached as if we are packaged, it's sometimes ineffective and inauthentic. Voice is a key element of personal branding, many clients and employers *are*, in fact, looking for a package that they know, like and trust. You are a brand whether you know it or not.

When you're starting out, it's critical you focus on your audience and your message and be consistent in it. You have to commit to it and be that trusted advisor who's always there and can be counted on. Daily, weekly, biweekly, monthly – whatever it is. If you just take 15 minutes each day to do this, you will be surprised at what happens. For most people, the easiest place to cut from is your TV time, or move some of that digital media consumption to some digital media production!

Don't just start whipping out a bunch of content just yet. Buckle down, do your research, and create a plan to build your brand mania and start achieving that "Trusted Advisor Status" in your market.

There are two stages of creating a personal brand: defining and growing. If you do not define your brand in the first place, then it will not resonate with your audience as it grows. However, it doesn't matter how well-defined your brand is if you don't gain a following. Growth begets growth, and the larger your brand gets, the more that social proof will motivate people to jump on the bandwagon.

Let's take a look at building a brand with an eye to both of these factors to help you understand, start to finish, what it takes to build a brand people love and admire. Using some of the best examples across industries, we'll look at the exact steps you can take to create, build, and expand your brand for the life of your career – and beyond.

So, grab that notepad (take a look – I'm betting it has a well-known logo on the cover) and that pen (ditto), and let's get started.

Ditch the Idea That Brand is All About Looks

Let's get this out of the way right up front: a brand is more – way more – than some complementary colors and a logo.

Consider Houston law firm Jim Adler & Associates. Founded by Jim "The Texas Hammer" Adler in 1973, the nickname pretty much says it all. Jim Adler gets. It. Done. Adler's success is evident in the fact that the firm has now grown well beyond him, boasting more than a dozen attorneys within its ranks.

It's easy to see why. Think about that nickname for a minute; it packs more punch than any statistic about experience or expertise ever could. Certainly, no mere color scheme could convince an injured party to choose another business over "The Texas Hammer" just because they like blue hues.

This is a powerful example of what the word "brand" really stands for. It's not a look or even an attitude; it's a message of how you can help the people you want to help, whether they're businesses or individuals. Before you look at color schemes or contact your graphic designer, sit down, put your thinking cap on, and decide how you want to be known. Take some time and get into "your zone."

Stay True to Who You Are

One word: Authenticity. When first developing a brand, one of the most common mistakes people make is to target one of their heroes and try to be just like them. The problem with this is we often admire the qualities we *don't* have. It's great to aspire to be better, but hoping for a total change in personality is merely a route to madness.

So, stay true to yourself. If you are not The Texas Hammer, do not try to be The Texas Hammer. By which I mean: If you are not tough, but somewhat soft-spoken and warm, then The Hammer you are not. The problem with projecting a personality that isn't true to you is that soon enough, your client will discover the disconnect and when they do, they will more than likely walk away.

Show your clients the real you so that when you meet, they'll stick around. The importance of this congruence between who you are and who you portray yourself to be cannot be overstated.

Consider one of the most often-cited examples of personal branding: Tony Robbins. Probably the best-known motivational speaker worldwide, Tony Robbins is impressive for both his widespread name recognition and the depth of his message. He believes you can be anything you want, just as he is exactly what *he* wants to be. He is the most confident man on Earth. Period.

What is it you're confident about? What exactly are you, and what does that bring to your audience? Whatever it is, be that.

Focus on the one thing that you want to be known for and build on that. I met a woman at a speaking event recently who was a former VP of Marketing for Coca-Cola. She shared something with me that I have never forgotten: the best way to attract moths is with a focused beam of light. It really stuck and was ingrained in me, the power that a singular focus can bring.

Choose Who You Want to Serve

Don't attempt to be all things to all people. Have you picked a niche yet? Maybe it's B2B in small businesses, or if you're in the nutrition space, it's healthy, active people. Nope, that's still too broad. Try to go a layer deeper, and then maybe even a layer deeper after that. Subdivide the niche until you can't get any smaller. Dan Kennedy says there are "Riches in the Niches." It's time to zero in on the audience you want to attract.

I suspect people gloss over this because it requires some deep thought and isn't always easy, but guessing is not good when it comes to marketing, especially when the answers are at your fingertips – if you are willing to take the time and effort to look.

Let me introduce you to some great tools. If you're not already using Google Analytics, Search Console, and Facebook Audience Insights you should be. Proper research can be exciting, I promise! In fact, figuring out who makes up your audience might be the closest thing to picking up and counting the dollar bills that are falling from the money tree.

You have to "find your tribe."

Part of the problem here is that new entrepreneurs and business owners assume they have to figure out who "wants" them from a raft of potential customers that they are just randomly bumping into in the marketplace. While this is good and you can get an idea of what type of clients you serve, what might be more profitable is figuring out who you want to serve. Who is your tribe? Do you understand how they think? Do you speak their language? Brand yourself to attract your ideal customer. This is where the term "attraction marketing" came from.

Consider Chip and Joanna Gaines, the adorable and happily married couple behind HGTV's *Fixer Upper*. They have a very specific audience in mind: people who love beautiful homes, who enjoy seeing potential blossom, but who don't have the kind of money needed to call in a top-notch remodeling team. They can however, afford DIY projects and can do some of the remodel on their own. Once they hook people with their show, they can send them on to Magnolia Market, their trendy-yet-affordable e-commerce shop.

They know exactly who they want to serve...do you?

Your target audience is the group of people most likely to purchase from you and those you are in the best position to serve. Focus all of your attention on them and ignore the rest.

Create a Buyer Persona

The buyer persona is who your business would attract in your perfect world, and is also the audience you'll picture as you craft your story. Remember, your real-world customers may not all look exactly like the individual you highlight in your persona, but the aggregate should closely resemble the persona.

Look closely at the demographics of your most loyal customer base. Who utilizes your products and services? What do they desire most from businesses in your industry? These priorities may shift with time, but for now, surveys can provide a valuable snapshot of your role and your primary audience.

Ask consumers to fill out brief in-store questionnaires, or send surveys via email, or consider Google's new survey tool. Encourage honest feedback, leaving the opportunity not only to respond to multiple choice questions but also to provide long-form answers. You might be surprised by the responses. Many times you will find a different target audience when you dig into the data and see where the conversions and sales are coming from in your business.

In addition to sending out surveys, check your social media accounts and other online resources for feedback. Facebook Insights is excellent for this. Also, check out who tends to respond to your existing marketing efforts. Who takes the time to review your business on Yelp? These insights will grant you a closer look at the type of person who harbors strong feelings (good or bad) about your products and services.

Perhaps you're just getting started, and you're not sure exactly who your business will attract. Look at the makeup of your existing community, including the competition. Scour prospective competitors' marketing efforts and consumer feedback to determine who they attract and to see whether you can better appeal to an overlooked segment of their current market. Tools like Spyfu, SEMrush, SimilarWeb, and Alexa are listening tools that can help give you insight into what competitors are doing, where they are getting their traffic, and what is working for them.

As you draft your persona, include specific attributes. Highlight goals and motivations – what makes this semi-fictional person tick.

An excellent example of a buyer persona for a pediatric dentist:

Jennifer is a stay-at-home mom in her 30s. Jennifer desires to be a wonderful mother to her three children while also sticking close to her family's budget. As a prospective patient for a pediatric dentist, she prioritizes sanitary conditions, affordability, and quality service that will keep her children healthy now and in the months and years to come.

Her persona, or avatar, is simple, yet thorough – and it cuts to the crux of a pediatric dentist's target market.

Creating Your Buyer Avatar or Persona

To create an Avatar or a Persona (a profile of a specific client you want to work with):

1. Begin by listing demographic traits, such as sex, age, income, education level, marital status, and occupation.
2. Add information about your avatar's values, interest, and lifestyle. For example, does your avatar live a healthy or sedentary lifestyle? Does your avatar travel?
3. Name your avatar – this humanizes the avatar profile.
4. Find a photo that best represents your avatar.
5. Write a story about your avatar and how they discovered your products or services. How do they spend their day? How did they feel when they discovered you? Why did they feel that way? What problem does your product or service solve? How did they learn about your product/service? How did they feel after purchasing your product/service?

Your products/services will help solve some pain points your avatar is currently experiencing, and the resources and strategies you share will get them from where they are now to where they want to be.

You may have multiple avatars for your business, and these may evolve.

If you're struggling to define your avatar, begin by creating a negative avatar – customers who you don't want. Doing this will let you know exactly whom you don't want to work with and start narrowing down the audience.

The market you assume may be chomping at the bit to hear about your product or service may, in fact, be completely uninterested. Question why you gravitate to a particular persona, and then study your true market closer to determine if your assumptions align with reality.

Visit BuildYourBrandMania.com/Resources to download a worksheet to help create your own Buyer's Persona.

Develop a Unique Selling Proposition (USP)

For as long as we can remember, we've all jostled for a better position in the world. We want to outbid the competition and earn the attention of our prospects. It's human nature.

The problem is, it's hard to know where to start. Looking around, it seems like everyone else had the good fortune to stumble into a great business model, and you're still floundering. But while other companies' success might look sort of accidental from the outside, from within, they're usually quite methodical. And they know a secret that you may not, which is that one of the best means of grabbing and keeping the attention of your audience is to forge a *unique selling proposition*.

What is a Unique Selling Proposition (USP)?

A unique selling proposition is a basic guiding principle that helps you position your products or services in the marketplace. It is a finely-tuned offering to your clients or customers that no one else in the market can claim.

How Does Having a USP Help Your Business?

In a nutshell, your USP distinguishes you from the rest. It may mean you lose out on some clients and customers who don't align with your USP, but it will also bring in the right sorts of customers in droves – as long as the USP is clearly defined and useful to your audience. Let's look at an excellent case study.

What Does a Good USP Look Like?

An often-cited example of a great USP is Voodoo Donuts in Portland, Oregon. You might think donut shops are pretty standard: fry delicious dough, put frosting on top, charge money. To a certain extent, this is true, but the general popularity of donuts doesn't explain the fierce success of this donut chain.

They thought to themselves, *"How can we take one of America's favorite treats and turn it inside out? Despite the thousands and thousands of donut establishments across the land, how can we do something that no one has ever done?"*

The result is a hopping shop with a retro vibe, and the craziest sweets you've ever seen. You can get them in the shape of ghouls or monsters. They come in all colors of the rainbow. Buy them with sprinkles or Fruit Loops or M&Ms on top. Enjoy them with real, live strips of bacon sunk into maple frosting.

So what exactly is their USP? I'm guessing it's something along the lines of this: *We're going to make donuts people simply can't ignore. They'll be yummy and reasonably priced, but more than that, they'll be just plain FUNNY.*

How Can You Create Your Own Unique Selling Proposition?

Your USP depends heavily on your business. If you're a business coach, your USP might be that you'll see people at all hours of the day or night to accommodate those who have entrepreneurial schedules. Online teachers might offer their students a special tool that aligns with their courses, while a copywriter might promise to bring a unique brand of humor to the table. When developing yours, ask yourself:

- What's my business type?
- What do I do that the competition does not?
- How can I play that up even more strongly?
- How would I describe it?

How Do You Incorporate Your USP Into Your Marketing?

This is actually a pretty easy step. Once you have a well-crafted USP, it's simple to insert it into your marketing materials. Whittle it down to a single sentence – for instance, *24/7 coaching: help on your timeline* – to use on websites and business cards. Then flesh it out for about pages, brochures, and blog posts. Try to insert some version of it into everything you do, so that pretty soon, people won't be able to distinguish between *you* and your unique selling proposition.

When Should You Get Started?

Now you know all there is to know about USPs...at least on paper. The real learning won't begin, however, until you sit down and start thinking through what *your* unique selling proposition is. What can you give your customers that no one else does? How can you help them get to where they want to go, as quickly and effectively as possible?

These are the essential questions to ask, and you should give yourself plenty of time to answer them, so don't wait to get started. Don't expect to nail your USP overnight. In fact, it will likely develop over time, as you continue to serve your clients and customers, then use their feedback to narrow and enrich your services even further.

On the other hand, don't wait. Crafting and living by a strong USP is more likely to bring you success than any other single step, so get started today.

Go for It

While to a certain extent all of the steps here are development steps, we are now moving into the "growth" stage of brand building mania. You will continue to refine the basics, but you've established a great foundation and can now use it to get the word out. And that's precisely what it's time to do: Tell people all about your brand.

"But wait!" You're thinking, "I am not ready to shout from the rooftops yet. Don't I need to build a target client list, or get some more testimonials, or write a thesis on what my brand is before I'm ready to tell the world?"

Nope. Just make sure you're good at what you do. Don't be in too much of a hurry to market until you are good at what you do; otherwise, it will just speed up the rate at which everyone finds out how good or not good you are. Just start practicing in public.

This concept was made popular by one of my favorite online gurus, Seth Godin. Essentially Godin states that you can't get good at anything by toiling away at it in your safe little basement hideaway. To get noticed, you must emerge from your "Fortress of Solitude" and show the world what you've got; this is about getting out of your comfort zone. There is no perfect time; there is only now, and now is precisely the time when you need to start putting your brand into effect.

Learn to Network

We all think we know how to network, but the truth is, most of us aren't good at it. It's not enough merely to walk around shaking a few new hands and getting business cards at a cocktail party. Networking is difficult, time-consuming, and frightening, but it is *very* rewarding. Now more than ever.

Before, you could network and tell people what you do, and perhaps they would tell someone else, or pass your card on when services are needed. Today, though, the possibilities are almost limitless. First, there's the Internet.

Second, there's a thing called the Internet.

Third, did I mention the Internet?

The digital age has thrown networking into hyper drive, and for anyone savvy enough to make use of this, it's a *huge* boon. Facebook groups are endless networking events ready for you to jump into almost any topic. So now that you have a website, you can drive people toward it on Facebook and a variety of other social media platforms with a bit of digital hand-shaking and rapport building, just as if you were at a networking event. Also, remember you have to provide value first. Help the other person in some way before asking for something yourself.

Start with LinkedIn, which is hands-down the best online networking site for one simple reason: You have access not only to your network but also to everyone in your contacts' networks as well. Unlike other social media sites, people are on LinkedIn to do business-related activities. That makes it an appropriate place to connect about business.

When I was a recruiter, I spent eight hours a day, five days a week networking on LinkedIn. I was an early adopter when LinkedIn launched. It was pure networking gold, and it still is, just a little harder to mine right now with all the paid walls going up. LinkedIn has an "Ask for an Introduction" feature that enables you to reach out to one of your connections and ask for an introduction to one of their connections.

As long as you have a good reason for doing so, your mutual connection will usually be happy to introduce you. "Hi!" doesn't count, but a genuine query about an interest in an opportunity or an expertise request does. Don't be shy about sending out messages to your contacts and letting them know what you do, either. Chances are you can help them, or someone they know, one day. For help getting started, reach out to me at LinkedIn.com/in/MattBertramLive. I would love to connect with you and hear your feedback on this book.

Give Yourself Time

Finally, know that building a personal brand takes time. That's the reason people are always talking about "building" one, not "choosing" one. You don't just point at a brand and stick it in your pocket. You have to hone and shape it over time, add more content to refine and underline your brand, take feedback from your audience, re-hone, and re-shape.

Rinse and repeat.

Don't let a little bit of success derail you, either. Success can be just as dangerous as failure because it gives you a rosy glow that convinces you that you're doing okay, and you can stop building for a bit, and then things change, and you wonder why. Truly successful people never stop working to build and expand, and you shouldn't either. Be consistent in your efforts.

As you continue to grow your brand, reach out and network, see success and capitalize on it, you will eventually realize that your brand has started to build itself. At that point, all it needs is guidance from you to make it as impressive as it can be.

As you start to develop a memorable personal brand, more prospective customers will be paying attention to you and your business. You need to keep it up and capitalize on it. That leads us to the next chapter: *Storytelling*.

How to Win Over Prospective Customers by Telling Your Story

In today's digital world, it is easy for all of us to become desensitized. We have started to tune things out. Jay Walker-Smith from Kantar Consulting says we've gone from being exposed to about 500 ads per day in the 1970s to as many as 5,000 ads per day today. It's understandable that most marketing has lost its effectiveness. So, how do we get through all the noise?

Tap into your prospect's emotions! SCREAMING AT THEM COULD WORK, but that might not garner the right kind of attention.

Information may hold the express purpose of attracting new clients or strengthening customer engagement, but without a compelling backstory they will not connect, and your message gets forgotten. Think about it: what captures your attention? A jumbled list of statistics? Or a compelling plot? If you're like most consumers and something piques your interest, not only will you be far more eager to listen, you'll also remember the message long after.

Why is this? Because our brains make little distinction between an experience we are reading or hearing about and one that is actually happening. Our brain uses imagery to store information so those stats may briefly impress you now, but unless your brain believes it actually experienced something, it will be lost in short-term memory. Ample research indicates that consumers connect more closely with a message when it features elements of storytelling, rather than cold, hard facts.

Interesting, right? Marketing is, at its heart, just storytelling.

Each Facebook post, YouTube video, or promotional poster is another page or chapter in the ongoing saga of your life and business intertwined. If your target market connects with the story, they'll be eager to turn the next page; if at any point they get bored with your message, they'll search for more exciting content.

Your job is to keep them interested while staying true to your brand, and the use of stories is hands down the best way to do this. That's why there's no question that storytelling dominates in today's quickly-changing marketing sphere.

However, there's a vast difference between understanding the importance of a good story and actually telling one. The sooner you learn how to connect with your audience via storytelling, the better results you'll achieve in any given marketing campaign.

A lot of the time we try to *logically* convince everyone to see us as the best option for our product or services and we word vomit all over the place. We share studies, stats, and technical jargon. We love our sales pitch and know everyone should see it our way and hire us.

But all the logical stuff that strengthens belief will not help anyone unless they've had the same emotional experience you had. All that sales babble usually annoys people and flies right past them with no connection. You must get them to the same point as you emotionally so they can see what you see.

This applies to almost any large purchase or investment. Do people who buy SUVs necessarily go off-roading, making that thrilling mention of the four-wheel drive so practical, or are they buying an image, a feeling, a possibility? Do men buy $150,000 sports cars to race or to mock speed limits? Or are they merely chasing a dream?

Remember all decisions are emotional; logic helps people justify those decisions.

One huge tip I got from Russell Brunson, founder of ClickFunnels, is that when telling a story, you need to have your reader go on the "journey of transformation" with you. He calls this an Epiphany Bridge. It's merely a story that takes people through the emotional experience that gets them excited about the opportunity you are offering them. This means your audience must connect with you and where you were before you tell the story or parable that communicates whatever benefits you are trying to express so that they go on this journey with you.

The first time you discovered the power of what you now do for a living perhaps or something special that happened inside of you. You maybe had a powerful and life-changing emotional experience? Your prospects must go on the same journey and connect with you as you tell your story as they will look for similarities with the struggles in their own life.

For example, let's say that when I was a child, my little brother was hit by a car. He was okay but was in the hospital for a long time. I saw my parents not just worried about his health, but also about how they would pay the medical bills, and all the strain that was put on them. A lawyer got involved and won a massive settlement for our family. My parents were no longer stressed, and my brother got all the help he needed. The money also helped provide the capital for me to be the first in my family to go to college. This experience led me to law school, and I eventually became an attorney.

So, at this point in the story, you might be emotionally invested, and you can see how the experience influenced and shaped me, and now whatever I say next, you will probably be right there with me. This is the Epiphany Bridge that is effective in all types of storytelling.

For all of you now worried about my brother, this story was just for illustrative purposes and only meant to be used as an example. I don't have a brother, only a lovely sister, and she is fine. However, I am sure that this is someone's story out there. God bless.

Understanding Your Audience

The best story in the world will not emotionally connect with people in any way if it's told to the wrong audience and they are not receptive. Consumers need to be on board with the central theme of your story or not only will it fail to garner a response, but it will also harm the brand you've worked so hard to establish. Remember your target persona.

Few romance writers pepper their stories with continuous action sequences. They know that is not why people buy and read their books. They understand their audience and write to meet the unique demands of their readership. In business, knowing your audience can be a bit trickier. You have to get more granular and often think outside the box if you want to achieve success.

The Importance of Positioning

It often all comes down to positioning. Positioning is what makes you different, where you fit in the marketplace, and to whom you are appealing.

Think about the success of Old Spice's *The Man Your Man Could Smell Like* campaign. Before this marketing push, most people would have expected Old Spice to market to men between the ages of 40 and 60 – certainly not young women. At this time, Old Spice as a brand was on its heels. They were losing market share rapidly to Axe Body Spray, who was killing them in the youth market with the "Axe Effect" campaign. Remember, the effect was supposed to draw women in hordes to any male that sprayed it on himself. (I admit I was a customer at the time, the marketing worked on me.)

Old Spice's marketing agency was tasked to combat this, and careful research demonstrated that women held the real purchasing power in this unique market, with females buying a surprising 70% of male toiletries. Hence, the unexpected for Old Spice's next-generation audience: a young woman not entirely satisfied with her significant other's scent.

Old Spice exemplifies how an accurate understanding of a company's audience and the right persona can completely transform a brand. The goal of the campaign was to shift Old Spice's perception, thereby delivering a younger, hipper consumer base.

The effort proved wildly successful; before the YouTube marketing effort, most people thought of Old Spice as outdated and uncool. Within just 30 days of the campaign's launch, the company boasted over 40 million views on YouTube, and more importantly, a 107% jump in body wash sales. This shift affected the positioning of the brand and is recognized as one of the best marketing turnarounds of all time.

You have my permission to be a rebel, stand out, swim against the grain - you don't want to always fit in with what everyone else is doing. Is there an untapped audience in your niche, and how are you positioned to meet it?

The Importance of Presentation

The content of your story is important, but so is its presentation. Two people may look the same on paper but hold completely different perspectives. Likewise, an intriguing idea can take on an entirely new meaning based on its presentation. Be mindful of all elements of your story to avoid inadvertently giving your audience the wrong impression.

Word choice can make a huge difference. A perfect example: athlete versus jock. Technically, the two words hold similar meaning, and yet, they generate vastly different responses. An excellent resource for choosing the right word is the book *Words That Sell* by Richard Bayan.

Word choice certainly makes a difference for Hughes Media Law Group, in which Joleen Hughes draws on her ample experience in the music industry to get prospective clients excited. Her simple phrase "Lawyers Who Rock" tells a story all on its own, immediately differentiating Hughes Media Law Group from the competition.

Take this example from Apple:

MacBook. Light Years ahead.

We see here how the ad copy was able to condense all the features of the product in just three words. The lightness in weight is a given, but all the innovations and specifications are summarized by the phrase "Years ahead."

But don't only think about the text. No matter the role words play in your story, the visual presentation is essential too. Color, shadow, and focus all make a difference. Some consumers will respond to bright, cheerful images, while other stories benefit from something a bit more nuanced. There are some great resources out there on the psychologies of color in marketing. Google Images, "colors marketing" and there are some great infographics about the subject. I don't have a resource I use exclusively, and there is some debate on what different colors mean. However, I think it's always safe to go with some shade of blue. Blue universally represents trust and loyalty.

Visually, viewers should grasp the basic tenets of your story before they even read the caption. For example, in an evocative video from 'Texas Law Hawk' Bryan E. Wilson, viewers can easily identify the premise: a confident and aggressive criminal lawyer eager to defend his clients' rights. From brief clips on a motorcycle to background American flag images, the video immediately draws in viewers, identifies the target market, and provides a clear proposition. The caption provides valuable information but is by no means needed to understand the video's core message.

Spend time on this step. It might not be the most crucial element to your story, and it certainly won't be the one that closes the sale. But it is the one that opens the door of possibility and could close it. It gets people interested in your brand, and for that, it's worth getting right.

Conclude the Story with a Call to Action (CTA)

Like any good story, your marketing push should include conflict to attract viewers' interest. For example, Dollar Shave Club also does an excellent job of establishing conflict and resolution in its 2012 viral video *Our Blades Are F***ing Great*. In this simple, yet hilarious video, the company's founder quickly established a persona (young men unwilling to spend a fortune on razors) and wove a relatable tale of frustration with fancy, overpriced razors. Most importantly, however, Dollar Shave Club concluded that story with a clear call to action, inviting audience members to switch from the passive role of a viewer to an active role in the subscription company's rapid evolution.

Most businesses do not effectively use CTAs in their marketing. A CTA should elicit an emotional response from the reader to influence them to sign up for a program or purchase a product.

Many small businesses do not have a CTA on their website, or their CTA is not compelling enough for the reader to take action.

Here are a few basic examples of compelling CTAs that can be used to boost your marketing conversion rates:

- Click Here for Details
- Join Today to Receive a Bonus
- Start Your 7-Day Risk-Free Trial

- Apply Here, Deal Ends Today
- Request Your FREE Custom Quote

For millennia, humans have passed down knowledge and wisdom through simple, engaging stories. Today, those stories form the backbone of the world's most effective marketing campaigns. Learn to be a good storyteller and deliver a strong CTA, and you'll be well-rewarded with increased engagement, more sales, and impressive customer retention.

Now that you know how to tell a story with your marketing and get people to take action, let's look at how to leverage that with *Content Marketing*.

Content Marketing for Local Businesses - Establishing Yourself as the Local Authority

Imagine the types of businesses most likely to suffer during a recession. What comes to mind? When money is tight, and consumers are pulling in the reigns, logic says it's those luxury services for which they tend to stop paying. So, how could a pool and spa business not only avoid going under but thrive, during the recent recession? The answer may shock you.

Let's take a look at an example of how you might recession-proof your business by building your brand. During the most recent recession, Marcus Sheridan, owner of River Pools and Spas, realized he had a challenge. During economically challenging times, people just aren't going to buy new pools. He knew some consumers who would still spend money on this, and he knew that he had to be the company they chose when they decided to install a pool.

How would he do this? By becoming the local authority for the inground swimming pool market.

Marcus completely reinvented his marketing strategy. Instead of spending over $150,000 a year on radio, telephone and direct mail ads, the tried-and-true marketing platforms for his industry, he focused one-third of that budget on inbound marketing, including content marketing. His website traffic shot through the roof, and his leads increased over 400%. Most importantly, he had his best year in business, in the middle of a recession.

What, precisely, did Marcus do that contributed to this success? He embraced content marketing to the fullest. In a recent interview on Copyblogger, he said, "On our site, we literally answer every question a consumer could possibly have about buying a fiberglass pool. When the housing market collapsed in 2008, we were in big trouble. That's when we discovered content marketing and decided to be the best teachers in the world about our business – which was inground fiberglass swimming pools. This decision saved our company."

Unlike his competitors, Marcus learned and embraced the secret to success – establishing himself as the authority on his niche topic in his local area through the power of content marketing. This marketing secret is the key to skyrocketing the success of local companies of all types, from doctors' offices to real estate pros. If you can establish yourself as the local authority through the content you produce and distribute, you too can have the best year of your life in business.

How can you, too, find the type of success Marcus and River Pools and Spas had? Did he somehow get lucky, or is there a format to follow to replicate his results? The answer to these critical questions is this – any local business can replicate the type of success that Marcus had in good times and bad. Yes, you read that right – any business can do the same thing. How? By learning to leverage content to establish yourself as the local authority. Master this secret, and you will create your success.

What Is Content Marketing?

To establish yourself as an authority, you must understand what content marketing is: a marketing strategy that uses written content including articles, blog posts, and forum posts that provides useful information to the readers in your market. The material itself is helpful to the reader, but with the ultimate goal of converting the reader into a client, contact or customer.

As a local professional or service provider, you must establish yourself as a trustworthy leader in the field, and content marketing helps you do this. When the goal of your content marketing is to brand yourself as an authority, it can be called *authority content marketing*.

Authority content marketing not only focuses on providing useful information to the reader and nudging them to decide and take action, but it also focuses on branding you and your company as an authority on the subject.

For example, a doctor who regularly publishes health-related information in a blog that helps his patients take better care of themselves will be branded as knowledgeable in his field of medicine. When the patient needs help beyond what he can do at home, that doctor will be the first one he thinks to call.

Building an Authority Content Marketing Strategy

Now you know that the secret to skyrocketing success like Marcus had is doing authority content marketing, so you may be asking yourself, "How do I get started?"

First, you need to create an authority content marketing strategy. Unfortunately, far too many professionals jump on board the content train without taking the time to create a plan.

Establish Your Objectives

> *"All successful people have a goal.* No one can get anywhere unless he knows where he wants to go and what he wants to be or do.*"*
>
> — *Norman Vincent Peale*

You can avoid the pitfalls your competitors are falling into by creating a proven plan for your content marketing success. No content marketing strategy works without a goal, so setting a goal should be your first step.

Establish a S.M.A.R.T. goal:

Specific, Measurable, Acceptable, Realistic, Time-Bound. According to Forbes, five common goals for content marketing include:

- Building brand awareness
- Building brand loyalty
- Providing education for customers
- Improving customer engagement
- Encouraging recruitment of more talent

All of these goals can drive a content marketing strategy, but for the local business or the local professional, they fall short of Peter Drucker's SMART concept. While you may wish to educate your customers and engage with your clients, this will not prevent you from having to chase leads if you don't get specific and define them.

Your objective should be to brand yourself as an authority in your field. Define success with content marketing that is measurable and realistic and in an acceptable time frame. When you write down your goals, your subconscious mind starts moving you in that direction! I encourage you to do it. Most successful people I know have written goals. I write mine on my bathroom mirror each week with a dry erase marker. It helps me focus daily on what I need to accomplish that day or that week.

Example of Goal Setting That Worked

Before you say this won't work for you, or your business, listen to this particular example about carbon and stainless steel carbon tanks – a field that generally doesn't lend itself well to content people want to read. Fisher Tank is a full-service welded tank fabricator and constructor whose services include construction, design, engineering, and repairs of tanks.

The problem Fisher Tank faced was a long, expensive sales cycle that could last from 12 months to several years and run into millions of dollars. They would get projects from cold calling, referrals and repeat customers, but they needed a way to grow their B2B business.

Most specialty manufacturers don't use content marketing because they think their prospects won't search the internet to make this type of purchase, or they are not on social media. Fisher Tank decided to use a redesigned website to attract more qualified prospects, convert them to leads with content, and continue to nurture them with more specific content.

Fisher Tank's existing website had no social media links, no calls to action, no blog, and no social sharing abilities. The new site included simplified navigation, social media links for the business, and a blog. Expert advice, industry news, and tips were added regularly to the site, almost religiously. It was part of their process and on their "to do" list. Free resources, like white papers, were provided that linked to a lead generation page, which created awareness and provided education about their product. Each month, they would post a summary of all new content on their blog. Chris Burres calls this a "20-Mile March;" it highlights the power of compounding from a routine.

The results were staggering. Because a clearly defined goal backed the content, it was effective. In twelve weeks, overall web traffic increased 119%, traffic from social media increased 4,800%, lead conversions increased 3,900%, requests for quotes increased 500%, and the value of new qualified sales opportunities was $3.4 million!

What a "Conversion" Is to You

Most professionals want their blog and other content to turn into "conversions," but what exactly is a conversion? You must be able to define what makes a prospect count as a "conversion" to measure the success of your authority content marketing efforts. This definition will vary from one business or professional to the next, but it must be clearly defined.

For some industries, like plumbing or HVAC, a conversion may be having someone fill out the "Schedule a Service Call" form. For the medical field, a conversion may be someone clicking the "Schedule an Appointment" link and scheduling the appointment. A financial consultant or physical trainer may consider a conversion successful if someone signs up for a class, webinar or responds to an email from an email marketing campaign. For an e-commerce business, a conversion would be someone who makes a purchase online. As you can see, this definition will vary from one business, campaign, or professional to the next so you must clearly define it to measure your success.

When you focus on building your authority with your content marketing, you can view your success through shares and site visitors. You can also compare your sales from month to month to determine if you are getting more traffic and business through your content marketing efforts in a program like Hubspot. Also, take into consideration a multi-touch attribution model, jump into your Google Analytics data and the results may surprise you. I have seen customers return to a website or a blog upwards of eight times before buying and have a conversion window up to 90+ days.

Define Your Target Market Pain Points

Once you know what you want people to do (view you as an authority) and why you are investing time in your content marketing strategy (to brand yourself as the local authority), you must define your target market's pain points. Remember the personas we created for your ideal client? If you don't, take some time to think it through.

Your ideal client is someone who both needs and can afford your product or services. For example, if you are a family law attorney, your local community may have many people who could use your services. After all, people in all walks of life are going to need to seek help with perhaps a divorce, but those who can afford *you* are going to be in a very specific demographic. You want your marketing to attract your ideal candidate and repel those you don't want.

Enter the conversation that is already going on in your prospect's mind."

— Robert Collier, one of the greatest copywriters of the early 1900s

By getting inside your customer's head, you will understand the kind of problems they have and can offer solutions they are looking for, and you will be able to build content that will talk directly to them and their needs.

Roberts and Durkee was a Florida law firm that wanted to offer services to people who had been exposed to the health hazards of Chinese drywall. To do that, they needed to both reach those construction workers and homeowners who were exposed to toxic Chinese- manufactured drywall, and also educate them about why this was a problem. They created a website to provide this education which, in turn, made them into the local consumer advocates who were a trusted authority on the Chinese drywall problem. Soon, their target market, those affected by the toxic drywall, were coming to them for legal help, and their business succeeded.

Why were Roberts and Durkee successful? Because they clearly defined their target market needs – those affected by the Chinese drywall problem, and then marketed directly to them. The rest fell into place naturally. Unlocking the secret of authority marketing, and then targeting the *right* consumer, made them successful.

Lauren Luke is another example of this. To supplement her income as a taxi dispatcher, Lauren launched a side business selling makeup. Soon she realized that her target market –

women who used makeup –had a problem. They didn't know how to properly apply the products they were buying.

Because Lauren knew her target market and where they were struggling, she was able to create YouTube videos to help. She used the products she was selling and demonstrated how to apply them in makeup application videos. Soon sales went through the roof, and she was able to launch her own brand of makeup, which can now be purchased at Sephora. Her YouTube channel has a bigger following than Estée Lauder, and she never spent time marketing through traditional methods.

Both of these examples show the power of knowing your target market's problems and then creating content to meet a specific need they had. By doing so, you can quickly create that authority image you need for your success.

Content Is King

Your content should be like a BOMB – it should blow your audience's minds! Content can come in many forms: blogs, checklists, how-to guides, who's who books, product reviews, e-books, webinars, video courses, whatever you can think of that has value to your target market. The best place to put your content is everywhere, but keep it flexible so you can use the same story or topic on a PowerPoint presentation at a seminar, in a podcast sent to your client base, or even as a free report sent through your email marketing campaign. The more places you can use the content, the more valuable it will be, and the more authoritative you will appear. Once written, find an image or video to go with the content to make it more visually appealing.

You should be regularly creating new relevant content to post on your site so that Google will give the entire site more visibility and weight in the search and phrases for which you want to be indexed. Be deliberate in what you post and give your posts some length. Four-hundred to 500-word pages or blogs just won't cut it anymore; it's now considered thin content and Google doesn't like it. Try creating some comprehensive articles or lists about topics in your niche, or find articles that you like that rank well (an example would be "101 Plumbing, Tips, Tricks and Advice You Need to Know" published by Tiger Electrical Services on LinkedIn) and one-up them.

This is called "skyscraper" or "pillar" content because you're stacking so much information on top of each other. Try outdoing the best article in your niche, until it reaches the sky! Check out Brian Dean's or Neil Patel's blogs to better understand what I mean by skyscraper content as well. They are some of the best blogs I have ever read.

Admittedly a lot of us are always looking for those magic silver bullets to bring more website traffic and sales to use without all the work, but blogging and social sharing are necessary to provide a venue for you to showcase your expertise. Through your articles, comments, videos, and guest posting, you give back to the community.

Easier said than done, right? Who has the time? I have found that videos work best. There's just nothing better for increasing time on page and engagement with your website than video content. YouTube has a great YouTube Creator Academy to help you grow your channel with guided lessons and courses.

If your favorite medium is writing, I would suggest going through Digital Marketer's *Social & Community Manager* course to get a solid foundation and leverage your blog posts into social posts that will drive traffic back to you through a process known as "splintering." The course was helpful to me when I was getting started. Make sure you get the course on sale or do the free trial, or better yet, beg Ryan Deiss to give you access! (Just kidding, that probably won't work.)

Also, when sharing content on social media, consider the platform or channel that you are on, and know that people consume information differently. Some people like links, pictures, or videos, while some like text. Make sure you speak to different people in different ways.

Also, remember to create content that is fun to digest. Infotainment is the name of the game. People want to be informed, but they also want to be entertained. The average attention span of an American is hovering around about eight seconds. A goldfish has a longer attention span than most Americans! Crazy, right? If this fact resonates with you as it did for me, you might like to explore this topic more. *Amusing Ourselves to Death* by Neil Postman is an interesting read.

Fight Writer's Block

If you have been reading this and in the back of your mind content creation still feels overwhelming, don't stress. Just document what you do. Document your day-to-day, what steps you go through, your thought process, and why you do things in what order.

Don't think of it as creating content; think of it as documenting your process through writing or video recording. It's that easy!

Have you found yourself staring at an empty computer screen, feeling like that blinking cursor is mocking you? One of the best ways to beat writer's block is to have a swipe file of stuff others have created that you liked. File these away as a running list of ideas/thoughts that you always have with you. Whether it's in a notebook you put into your purse or briefcase or an app on your phone, have a place to jot down ideas as they come to you. Some common places to pick up ideas for articles and blog posts include:

- News items relating to your area of expertise
- Conversations with clients or customers
- Successes you have seen in the industry
- Movies that relate to your industry
- Blogs from other professionals in different geographic areas
- Mistakes you have made or seen
- Things you choose to learn about because you don't know

Make sure your ideas are unique, as this will help your content stand out as authoritative. Don't just recycle the same ideas others have had; but come up with topics that are unique to you and your target market. Keep a running list of ideas, and when the time comes to write, you will always have something to pull from.

I would also recommend hiring someone to help with this, as I even have trouble with it myself. You could chat with an experienced content creator like my peeps at eWebResults, which has been in business since 1999. The eWeb team boasts full-time copywriters, social media marketers, and SEO'ers on staff. Or you could use something like Textbroker to help bridge the gap if you want to keep it in-house.

Start to Promote

If content is king, distribution is queen.

Once you've written and published your content, you need to get eyes on it. Many professionals use social media for this. According to the LinkedIn Technology Marketing Community, LinkedIn is the most effective social media platform for delivering content, with 82% effectiveness, followed by Twitter at 66% and Facebook at 41% (LinkedIn, 2014). Utilizing all three will help get your content out there, and the platform on which your target market spends the most time is likely the most effective for your needs.

Okay, so now you hopefully have some great content but how will you get anyone to see it? You can distribute your content or pieces of your content on social media or paid ads with the click of a button. You can push this content to all your digital properties through tools like IFTTT (If This, Then That), Hootsuite, or Buffer to increase your digital footprint and lead prospects back to your site. I am not going to go into detail about using IFTTT, duplicate content, or even social bookmarking as there is a lot of debate on these topics, but if you email me, I will send you some of the IFTTT recipes I use and tell you how I am implementing these strategies.

Social media is just the first place to look to promote your content. Some lesser-known, but still effective, options include:

Quoting Experts – Whether you ask for a quote that's not found elsewhere or find a quote online to put into your content, citing experts will help more people read what you've written. You can mention those experts when you publish your pieces, and having quotes from established experts will make your work more effective at establishing you as an authority as well.

Content Communities – Content communities are websites that allow you to submit your content to help grow your audience. Find communities where you can submit content along with a bio for the most effectiveness. The more places you are published, the more of an expert you appear to be. Make sure the content you publish elsewhere is quality content in line with your branding goals.

Guest Blogging – Guest blogging on niche sites where your topic is regularly discussed will help brand you as an expert. For local businesses, finding sites that target your local market is the most effective. Consider guest blogging on the local news station blog or community events website. Link to your blog to drive more traffic to your site, if allowed.

Connect with Influencers – One of the best ways to use your content to establish yourself as an authority is to have others quote you or share your content. Use LinkedIn to establish relationships with influencers in your industry. Build those connections, share their content, and then ask for a return favor. If you can get a mention by one of the best in the industry, people will start viewing you as an expert as well.

Encourage Social Sharing – Social sharing is the phenomenon that occurs when your readers share your content through social media. This is a powerful way to get your local community to view you as a trusted authority. For example, if you are a landscaping company and someone shares your helpful article on tree and shrub maintenance, and their neighbor sees the article, your name will be the first considered when that neighbor is in need of lawn help or tree removal. When encouraging social sharing, focus on Facebook, which accounts for over half of all social sharing done across the globe (Statista, 2016). We can talk about "Growth Hacking" and how to trip the virality algorithms to hockey stick your user engagement growth in the next book or in a one-on-one coaching session.

Leverage Review Sites

"Nothing draws a crowd quite like a crowd."

– P.T. Barnum

88% of consumers trust online reviews as much as personal recommendations (MDG Advertising, 2014). Wow! If that is not an influencing factor, I don't know what is! Our minds process so many decisions each day, so our brains are always looking for shortcuts. Reviews are shortcuts. Finding "A Trusted Advisor" that we can put our faith in and not need to think or make a decision, is another.

Reviews and testimonials from fans say what you cannot. If you have a business, ask for reviews! Ask customers when they are the happiest and when they might refer business to you. Positive reviews are critical in this process and need to be collected along the way.

Customer testimonials and endorsements send strong trust signals because they're candid endorsements of your product or service by people who have used it. Your customers' words will always be more persuasive than your own. Ask them to talk about how you helped them solve their problem so others with similar problems will know you can help them as well. Video testimonials are the best if you can get them. Written testimonials are also good too, but try to include a photo, if possible, to enhance credibility. If you still think this is too much work or too daunting, consider using a service like *Trustpilot* or *Magnfi* to help generate reviews.

Some of the best places for reviews include:

Google My Business – This is one of the most accessible places a customer can leave a review. More than 50% of people search for businesses while still logged into their Google browser which makes it seamless to leave a review of your business. Google loves companies with lots of reviews; it's a sign that the company is relevant and provides an excellent product or service which helps with your rankings quite a bit. You should also respond to reviews and start a conversation with your customers. A quick response can help build customer loyalty so be sure you are set up to receive alerts when a review is added about your company. *Note: If you do get a bad review, respond publicly and then take the conversation offline ASAP.*

Facebook Business – Facebook Business reviews can be a valuable form of social proof for any business. Facebook has a "star" rating system that allows customers to share their experience with others. These ratings encourage customers to rate businesses, which then makes the business appear in the news feed helping readers discover new businesses. Also, this enables businesses to create greater brand awareness.

Yelp – Yelp requires accurate information for your listing, and it also must have reviews. Yelp reviews come up high in the search engines, so be proactive about properly asking for reviews and responding to reviews or Yelp will hide them. You have been warned. Make sure reviews are posted in places to improve your reputation. I will let you be the judge as to "where" and "how" to create the most effective reviews for your business. Yelp is not my favorite.

LinkedIn – LinkedIn has powerful recommendations. Ask for recommendations from those you've worked with in the past and you will be proactively building a positive reputation. LinkedIn is a great place to easily collect references and reviews, especially if you are in a sales role.

There are hundreds of more review directories that I did not discuss like Bing Places, Whitepages, BBB, and more. Here is a list of the top 100:

Vndasta.com/blog/top-100-online-business-directories

Remember, the more positive things others are saying about you, the better your overall online reputation will be. Unfortunately, many times happy customers don't think to leave a review. However, if you ask for a review, many will be glad to provide one. Typically, seven out of 10 consumers will leave a review for a business when asked to do so!

Remember, in authority marketing, the more people who are talking about you, the better your reputation as "A Trusted Authority" in your local community. Use your content to become the trusted resource people turn to, and your business will grow.

Evaluate Your Efforts

After you've planned for, created and published content, you need to evaluate how successful it has been. Has your content branded you as an authority and helped grow your client base? Ask yourself questions like:

- Did your content achieve the conversions you outlined?
- Did your audience engage with and share your content?
- Did your content create the feeling of trust you needed?
- Were you successful in reaching your main objectives?
- Were you successful at driving *local* traffic to your site?
- Where does your content place in the search results?

After answering these questions, you should have a clear idea of whether or not you were successful. If you were successful, great! Keep doing what you have been doing. Most of the time, you are going to need to tweak your efforts after your initial evaluation, and that's fine. Remember, authority content marketing is constantly changing, so you are going to need to adjust and evaluate over and over again until you find what works for your business and your local market.

Case Study - The Bernie Sanders Campaign

Let's take one more look at someone who used the idea of authority content marketing effectively. Consider, as an example, the Bernie Sanders presidential campaign. Though he didn't win the presidential nomination, Bernie Sanders did succeed in branding himself as a political powerhouse. How? He utilized content marketing expertly. Regardless of how you lean politically, there are lessons here that you can learn from him.

During the 2016 presidential campaign, Sanders was found everywhere. He was on Instagram. He was blogging. He was emailing. He was on Twitter. He was on YouTube. He was on Facebook. And, while many of his competitors were also on these sites or doing these actions, he was doing it differently. Instead of playing up his credentials and shooting down his opponents, he was talking about his stand on the issues as he saw them. He got to the meat of the issues surrounding the campaign and got the conversation back to the problems the country was facing.

His website showcased the power of his content marketing strategy. He broke down the issues into 22 critical points. Each of those points had a full page including statistics, graphics, videos and a synopsis of his stand on that particular issue. It was evident that Sanders was an authority on each topic presented on his website.

This worked phenomenally because Sanders was able to get his target demographic on board. While he didn't win the election, he did win the hearts and minds of the millennial generation, and for a good reason. Millennials are the ones who research through blogs and social media, and this was where he distributed his message. Millennials also hate hype and self-promotion, so his strategy of turning himself into a trusted expert spoke right to what they wanted. He built trust, and people responded with donations and votes.

So how does this apply to you as you seek to brand yourself as "The Trusted Authority"? Since you are running a business and not a political campaign, can you follow in Bernie Sanders' footsteps? While your goal may be different, you can learn some valuable lessons about branding yourself through content by watching his success.

The Bernie Sanders campaign clearly shows two things.

1. Content can and should brand you as an authority. If you use it well, you can build trust with the power of content.
2. Content will only brand you as an authority if you meet the needs and expectations of your target audience.

This is why defining your target audience and then writing content for them is critical to branding yourself as an authority.

Creating a content marketing plan that positions you as the local authority can be done with the right strategy. By following these steps, you can increase your success while encouraging more people to contact you when they need the services you provide. If you are ready to stop chasing leads and to start positioning yourself as a leader, embrace these content marketing strategies!

Get Free Media Coverage to Establish Celebrity

We live in a world obsessed with celebrities. I'm not saying it's right; it's just the way it is. It doesn't matter who your target market is; they are fascinated by celebrities, and that trend isn't going to change. It's only growing.

People often confuse celebrity with credibility. Look no further than the wildly successful 1984 TV ad by Vicks 44 Cough Syrup. Actor Chris Robinson portrayed Dr. Rick Webber from the daytime drama *General Hospital* for the TV ad, coining the phrase, "I'm not a doctor, but I play one on TV."

One of the quickest ways to elevate your celebrity status is through the power of association. Being friends with celebrities within your niche can undoubtedly boost your celebrity factor.

If you don't know any, start interviewing other successful people in your industry like Napoleon Hill author of, "Think and Grow Rich" or Darren Hardy with *Success Magazine*. You could achieve celebrity status yourself. *(Actually, I recently meet Darren Hardy at a conference for business and executive coaches. If you want to learn the mechanics of how to sell from the stage, he is excellent.)*

Also, here is a "pro tip:" try to find a reason to get in the news. One of the best ways is to use Helpareporter.com (HARO) to comment on stories and be a local resource for young reporters that are always searching for quotes and stories in the 24-hour news cycle in which we live.

Content Marketing will make you famous! The more prolific you are in producing high-value content, the faster it will happen. Continue to write articles and start giving talks wherever you can and become active in industry and community events. By turning your growing personal brand and expertise into a celebrity, you will dominate your competition.

Using low-cost advertising in local newspapers, magazines, and paid campaigns on social media draws attention to you, enhances your brand, and increases your credibility, making the decision easier for prospects to choose you.

As the owner of a small, professional business, such as an accounting office, veterinary clinic, or doctor's office, you take on many of the responsibilities that employees would handle in a larger company. One of those responsibilities is that of marketer and media relations specialist. No matter what type of business you run, getting your name out there in front of potential new customers, vendors, and contacts is vital if you want to grow and thrive in today's competitive marketplace.

While traditional marketing activities and advertising are an excellent and accessible way to spread the word about your business, have you ever really considered the importance and possibility of gaining media coverage as a concerted, ongoing effort?

Yes, traditional marketing is much easier and does its job at getting your name out there, but it's expensive, and everyone is doing it.

Do not overlook the exposure and effectiveness of newspaper, local television news, and even radio mentions about you or your business. Also, intermingling the two can have an interesting effect. One example that people in the Houston, Texas area will immediately recognize is Mattress Mack. In the 1980's, Mattress Mack, or Jim McIngvale, spent his last $10,000 on advertising for his struggling Gallery Furniture store and placing himself as the actor in all the commercials. While the immediate goal was more sales, he became a semi-celebrity around Houston and has remained in the news and on the minds of residents by being involved in numerous fundraisers and community events around town. Even today, he is giving back to the community that kept him afloat during the lean times. You are now seeing others, like the President of H-E-B Houston, Scott McClelland, following suit due to its effectiveness.

Do people even follow traditional news outlets anymore?

You've probably heard talk that people don't read or watch the news anymore. There are plenty of statistics out there that support this. Pew's 2016 report showed declining viewership of local news in nearly every market. I, however, disagree with the premise. People still care about what is happening locally. They still read the news; it's just how and where people consume news that has changed. Many people do not sit down and watch the evening news or read the daily newspaper like they did many years ago. Although older Americans, such as the baby boomers, do still watch television news – more and more people are starting to "cut the cord" and stream their news and shows online. People still get their news from local sources; they just go about it differently today than they did in the past.

Many news channels have active accounts on social media networks, including Twitter, Facebook, Instagram, and LinkedIn. These accounts have a huge following and many people who never sit down and watch a newscast or read a paper follow the news through these feeds. As of August 2017, approximately 2/3 of Americans report that they get at least some of their news from social media networks – and this number keeps rising.

Social media is easy to follow from mobile devices, so the top news stories are caught during a commute or on a lunch break. Plus, social media is accessible 24 hours a day, seven days a week. Most of the news networks also have a website where they post articles and videos several times each day. You may even find live newscasts on streaming sites like YouTube, Facebook Live, and Periscope. Yes, traditional viewership may not be the same as it once was, but it does still exist–and could be a valuable resource for you.

So, what opportunities does local news coverage provide for you – a small business owner?

Since people are still tuning in to get local news coverage in one way or another, there is a captive audience who may be looking for a business just like yours – and they may not even know it yet.

Look at how effective news coverage can be for a small business. In Houston, Rye 51, a clothing store, donated brand new clothing from its shelves and collected from other retailers to provide it to first responders in the wake of Hurricane Harvey. The story was picked up by numerous news outlets and gave the store a much-deserved moment in the limelight.

A Facebook post about Sake Sushi Bar and Lounge in Port Arthur, Texas – which cooked over 1,000 meals for victims, first responders, and other volunteers after Hurricane Harvey – went viral. The post was shared over 444,000 times and received over a million interactions. The story was picked up by local and national media outlets and generated 5-star reviews for the local business.

Get Local Media Attention for Your Company

How can you obtain local media attention and put your company in front of these eyes? The process isn't always straightforward and can vary depending on your connections and what you have to offer. Here are a few tips to help you get started.

Utilize Social Media for Outreach

If the local news networks are already using social media, why not reach out via these same accounts to get attention for your cause? You may not only want to reach out on the network's social media accounts but also reach out to the journalists themselves who have their own accounts. As you do this, it is vital that you utilize proper etiquette. Thinking about etiquette will make it more likely that you get a positive response (or any response at all.) Don't be too pushy with them, politeness always wins.

Make sure that you are only contacting appropriate contacts about a story that may have local interest. For instance, it will probably not be effective to talk to the meteorologist about the basketball tournament that your clinic is sponsoring. Reach out to local reporters via direct message their social media accounts.

Muckrack's Media Outlet Directory is a great place to start (muckrack.com/media-outlets). They have a massive list of journalists, their beat, social media accounts, and more.

Also, before you reach out and ask for assistance, why not do something for the network or the journalists? Reporters are grateful for the businesses and active profiles that take the time to share their stories and drive traffic to the network. Doing this may put you in a favorable position with the right person before you even make the first contact and give you something of value to share. It's tough in a 24-hour news cycle for reporters always on the hunt for newsworthy stories.

If you do not get an immediate response from your local news network, remember that Facebook, Twitter, LinkedIn and other sites are crawling with bloggers and other less-known members of the media. You may make a connection you never expected and get some excellent coverage this way. Finally, never be a pest. You will not get a good response if you go overboard with your pitches or direct messages.

Ask for Additional Coverage

If you do happen to get in touch with a reporter who is willing to post a story on the local news channel's social media account, their website, or even a television newscast, make sure you are doing everything you can to take advantage of the opportunity. Ask if there is a way that producers can include your story in an email blast or newsletters. These follow-ups may help you get long-term benefits from your initial story, and it will put your name in front of even more potential customers. (Always ask for a link back to your site as well because this will help your SEO.) Securing additional coverage isn't always a possibility, but it's one of those instances where it certainly doesn't hurt to ask. Any additional coverage you gain will help build authority in your field – the importance of which cannot be overstated.

You may be able to create additional coverage by sharing your story with related groups, pages, and profiles using social media. By making an effort to boost readership (or viewership), you are doing a favor to the news outlet that helped you, and you are increasing the number of people who see your story.

Local Radio

Another way to help build authority and get your name out there is to get involved with your local radio station. According to NewsGeneration.com, 93% of people listen to AM or FM radio and audiences are more diverse than ever before in regards to age, race and income levels. While you may not think of radio as being as much of a big deal as TV, when it comes to reaching an audience, radio is huge.

If you are having a big event, invite a local radio DJ or radio personality to attend. Having someone from the station on site can offer a huge promotional boost. You may get your company mentioned on air, plus just having the DJ on hand during your event will make the day much more fun for everyone who attends and will attract additional attention. The radio appearance is a win-win situation for many organizations.

Just like any other pitch, make sure you are following proper etiquette and make sure that you have a newsworthy story for the DJ to cover. Your topic must be appealing to the radio station's target audience, or they will usually not want anything to do with it. Finally, when you do submit a pitch, make sure you're sending your idea to the correct person. In radio, this is usually the program producer rather than the on-air personality.

Newspaper

The local newspaper is often a popular option since it includes news targeted to the local audience that may not be found elsewhere. That's why it is vital to make contacts with this media source. Here are some tips that can lead to success with these publications.

- Get in touch by email. Include a press release with all the relevant facts included.

- Include an image when you submit your press release. If you have a digital camera or a smartphone, you should be able to capture a quality image. Identify any persons visible in the photo.

- Reporters receive many emails each day, so you want to follow up with a phone call to ensure your email has been received, and answer any questions the reporter may have.

- Newspapers are always looking for stories with a human interest angle. For example, a pizza parlor in Houston got media coverage when it shined a light on the costs associated with treating a child with type one diabetes. A mortgage assistance company gained national attention when the owner paid off the mortgage of a local struggling waitress.

- Submit informational and fundraising events that are open to the public to local news community calendars. Many Newspapers, TV stations, and entertainment websites have community calendars. Be sure to submit your event at least two weeks in advance to allow enough time for the event to be added to the website.

- After a successful event, share one or two high-quality photos with a short description of the event. Always include a call to action – such as a URL or phone number.

- Submit Letters to the Editor.

- Did you have a successful fundraising event or drive? Send a short thank you to your local papers. Tell readers about the success, and let them know there are still many ways they can help out.

More Tips

Work on Your Pitch – Reporters on TV, on the radio and even for newspapers are constantly inundated with story ideas from people just like you. The majority of these ideas are unusable or undesirable. When the pitches are focused only on the benefit of the business or individual who sends it, the idea is not likely to be accepted.

Once you've determined that you have a viable pitch, you need to do something to make it stand out from the dozens or hundreds of other pitches. Consider hiring professional assistants when writing a pitch. Even though there may be an upfront cost for this, the result can more than pay for itself. If you cannot hire someone, remember to make your pitch unique, while keeping it concise. Something that is too wordy will be more likely to get cast to the side.

Think Small – When you first start seeking media coverage, you may not get featured on the evening news. That's okay. As a local business, why not focus on local publications and other media avenues that have an impact on the people around you. Is there a neighborhood newspaper? What about a small magazine targeted to your industry? Getting featured in one of these could be the first step you need to get the broader coverage you desire. Also, don't overlook locally-based online platforms. There are many great blogs today that have a readership that rivals the standard local papers. Also, check out the video options online as well. People are doing amazing things on YouTube, Periscope, and Facebook live feeds. These online news sources produce pieces that you'll find are easier to share with your followers too.

Write a Press Release – The press release has evolved over the past decade. No longer is it used primarily to let print publications know about something in the hopes that they will circulate a story about you. Now, press releases are used to influence the search engines. Publishing a carefully crafted SEO press release through a service that distributes to the major news affiliates will get your company's information at the top of the search engines. Not only that but if the distribution is picked up by affiliates of NBC, CBS, ABC and the like, you will have some of the top websites in the world publishing positive information about you. PRWeb.com is great for this.

A press release may look complicated, but it is a relatively simple document that you can format using a template. Writing a press release yourself makes you take stock of exactly how newsworthy your event or "news" really is and may help you find additional angles you never considered. Crafting a well-written press release makes the reporting job much easier on a short-staffed small newspaper or other local publication which puts your pitch ahead of the other pitches out there. Include your name, address, and phone number in the press release. Google counts it as an unstructured citation or a NAP (Name, Address, Phone Number) listing.

Follow Up –You must realize that local news media networks, newspapers, and other outlets receive hundreds of pitches monthly or even weekly. What are you going to do to stand out from the crowd? Following up is an easy way to make sure you get noticed. Sending a simple email or calling a couple of weeks after submitting your pitch can get your pitch moved to the top of the stack or get someone to take a second look. If you are turned down, do not become an annoyance. Make sure you reconfigure your pitch before you try again. You may also find that a different news outlet is a better fit, so check out the other options available to you. If you go about it the right way, following up can be beneficial to you, without making you appear over-eager.

It's Easier Than You Think

Securing press coverage at a national level is difficult and may not have the benefit that you imagined it would. However, if you make the right contacts locally, it may be easier to reach a regional audience than you think. Radio stations, television studios, and newspapers are always looking for local interest stories and want to do what they can to make their communities seem like a great place to live, work and visit.

By thinking local with your media coverage goals, you will be reaching the people that are most likely to react favorably and who may one day become your customers, and you are building your authority with those same folks. Just remember that building a media profile may take some time. Don't be disappointed if you do not experience success overnight.

Finally, remember that media coverage is only one small part of your marketing plan, so don't become frustrated if things don't go your way right away. The most important thing is not to get discouraged if your ideas are not accepted immediately or if journalists and producers ignore your first pitches. Just be persistent and willing to learn from your mistakes. In doing this, you will eventually get the results you desire.

How to Reel in Your Lead with Landing Pages

You have landed an interview or guest article and contributed some great content into the online world! People have found you, and they are hooked... So how do you reel them in?

Digital marketing is a lot like fishing. A landing page is the place where you catch your online visitors and turn them into leads. Leads then convert into sales.

Many businesses fail to embrace the power of the landing page or fail to use them effectively if they have them. According to HubSpot, studies have shown that business websites with 10-15 landing pages typically increase conversions by 55% over business websites with less than ten landing pages. Businesses with more than 40 landing pages increase conversions by over 500% (Hubspot)!

Imagine if your business had 500% more prospects than it does right now. What would your sales projections look like?

What Is a Landing Page?

A landing page is a mini website that your visitors land on that has one purpose – to get the visitors to take action. Typically they would find you through your online marketing efforts whether it's an online search, a newsletter link, something you post on social media or even paid traffic, the result is the same: to "squeeze" the visitor for contact info. Landing pages can also be in the format of a long form sales letter that becomes your digital salesperson through emotional headlines and copy, overcoming objections with testimonials and guarantees, and pressing visitors by creating a sense of urgency in hopes they will buy. Think of the landing page as your digital sales professional working 24/7 on your behalf. Spend some time with it, consider even using a tool like Lucky Orange or HotJar to test the usability and see where people are getting tripped up and you are losing the conversion.

How to Use a Landing Page Effectively

How can you use a landing page effectively? The key is to provide the exact information the visitor believes he or she is searching for based on the place from which the visitor clicked to travel to your landing page. Your landing page needs to be interesting, targeted, and specific. Here's an example.

Emery Brett Ledger is a California lawyer who founded The Ledger Law Firm. Since 1998, Ledger has been offering personal injury and wrongful death legal services in California, and he uses landing pages to generate leads. According to Ledger, "Sometimes, a better-looking site isn't always as effective." To support his marketing efforts, he created the main firm website that works to build client trust and his overall brand.

For lead generation, he has several landing pages with effective calls-to-action and large intake forms. Each is connected to the specific traffic generating venue used. Ledger on the Law is one such example, and it's connected to Ledger's radio show. It stands alone from the informational site, with a prominent video and call-to-action that generates leads for the site.

According to Ledger, "There's always a problem when you make a site too informative. The user will come in and read and read and read and self-help their situation and won't reach out to the lawyer."

The art of landing page is to give your prospects just enough to see your expertise and understand that you can help them solve their problem.

Tools for Creating Landing Pages

How can you create a landing page? You can hire a web designer to handle the job, or you can tackle it on your own. Here are some common tools to use for creating user-friendly landing pages:

Unbounce – This is the tool my agency uses. It has templates and is effective for quick A/B through the drag-and-drop functionality and duplication features. One drawback to using this is there is no responsive logic in the placement of elements when building the mobile version. This is good and bad. You just have to build a desktop version and a mobile version separately, but it does give you more customization.

ClickFunnels – Great for sales funnels and long form sales letters to sell information products, consulting, or different services. This is Russell Brunson's company and is built to cater to the Direct Response marketer. I consider this product to be the evolution of Infusionsoft.

Thrive Themes – I love this product, and they have done a lot to improve the product since I began using it. There are a lot of the same bells and whistles that ClickFunnels has, but instead of $100 per month, you can buy each product and add-on or just pay ~$300 per year for the full suite. If you are getting started and cash flow is an issue, this is a good option to keep your spending down.

LeadPages and **Instapage** I've not had much experience with either, but I have heard great things about these products including their easy-to-use setup templates. You might want to consider these as well.

Find a tool that fits your needs and matches your level of technical and design knowledge, and start crafting landing pages that will convert traffic into leads.

Common Landing Page Mistakes

Before you get to work creating your landing pages, you will want to consider some common mistakes that marketers make with these pages. By avoiding these mistakes at the outset, you'll be able to avoid wasted costs and time. I like to think of landing pages as if someone was pushed out of a plane and parachuted into an unknown land and they have no idea where they are. Your goal is to help them understand as quickly as possible where they are and what to do next.

Mistake 1 - Skipping the Five-Second Test

You have about five seconds to capture your visitor's attention and turn them from traffic into a lead. Your site has to grab that attention quickly. To test your site, consider asking someone who is not connected to your business to view your page for five seconds, close the page, and then tell you what the page was about. If they are unable to tell you exactly what you're trying to convey, then you need to adjust the page. Ensure each element on the page conveys what you're trying to say so that the page can pass the five-second test.

Mistake 2 - Being Too Needy

Are you asking your visitors for too much? Are you asking for name, phone number, address, age, and email? That's too much. Your landing page needs a call-to-action that asks for as little as possible. Each additional field you ask for reduces your conversion rate by 23% or more. I recommend you default to as few fields as reasonably possible. You want the minimum amount of friction or resistance to them filling out your form. If you need to collect more information, create a multi-step process to acquire this information. Remember, your visitors don't want to give up their personal information, so the more you ask for, the less you will get.

Expedia found this to be true when setting up their lead capture forms. The company's original landing pages asked visitors for a Company Name which would apply to business visitors but not visitors traveling for personal reasons. This confused people and caused many to avoid the forms altogether. When they eliminated this unnecessary field, they saw a $12 million increase in profits as more users completed the registration and eventually made a purchase!

Mistake 3 - Headline and Content Offer Don't Match

Your headline and content on the landing page must match the wording on the ad that led people to click on the ad in the first place. If you're advertising "Android smartphones" but the link leads to an offer for "Samsung smartphones," even though the two are the same thing, you're going to lose some traffic. Use the same terms in the headline of the landing page that are in the ad to avoid confusing your visitors. Remember, visitors only have a five-second attention span, and that's barely enough time to realize that you are, indeed, offering what you say you're offering.

Mistake 4 - Poor Graphics

The graphics on your page need to be attractive, personal, and consistent with what you offer. If the image isn't relevant, it will create confusion. If it's a stock photo, it will look fake. If it's too flashy or overwhelmingly large, it will take away from your overall message. Use graphics, but make sure they support what you are trying to say. I have found that putting an image of what they are going to get substantially increases conversion rates.

Mistake 5 - Poor Overall Design Aesthetics

Graphics are just one part of the overall look of your landing page. You need to ensure that the font, color scheme, and design flows well, naturally drawing the visitor to the call-to-action and intake form without distracting elements. Remember to use white space to draw attention to your page, and keep the color and graphics consistent except for the action button which needs to stand out. Try using a color wheel to select complementary colors.

Mistake 6 - Unclear Call-to-Action (CTA)

Finally, make sure your CTA is clear and easy to find. Having too many forms or too much clutter on the landing page will prevent people from seeing the CTA, which will hurt your overall effectiveness. Include only one offer and one action. Ask for what you want.

The Weather Channel learned this when they created a website with the goal of turning visitors into premium subscribers. By decluttering the landing page and creating a single action, they saw a 225% increase in conversion.

Creating a simple landing page can be challenging because you might be inclined to add more and more, but too much information or too many elements makes it difficult for visitors to find and respond to your call-to-action. However, it can work if you are using the long form sales letter approach. Remember, your landing pages should either go really long or be super short.

Elements of the Perfect Landing Page

Now that you know what *not* to do, what *can* you do to ensure your landing page will convert? These are the elements found on a perfect landing page:

Killer Headline

Your headline needs to grab attention, tell the visitor what you're offering, and be as concise as possible. This isn't always easy to do, but with the right headline, you will pique their interest enough to keep reading.

Persuasive Sub-Heading

Below the headline, include a sub-heading with more details that help create a sense of need.

Compelling Images

Carefully choose images that are directly connected to the offer presented on your landing page. Again, this is one of the most important features of any leading page. You will need to A/B test many different formats to determine what works best. Have a picture of what you are selling somewhere above the fold.

Here's a quick example of how landing page images made a difference. When 37Signals wanted to increase conversions on their Highrise product page, they tested many different pages. One had a simple white background. Another page included an image of a person which increased their signups by 102.5%.

Using people in ads seems to increase conversions by about 300%. Featuring more attractive people increases it even more. Have the person in the image looking at the visitor or looking at the action you want them to take because visitors will typically follow the eyes. I have found that original or real images convert better than stock photos.

Clear Explanation

Clearly explain what your product or service is and how it will benefit the visitor. The explanation may be included in your headline, subheading or even the content, but make sure it's clear and easy to understand with a user-centric focus.

Value Proposition

People aren't going to give up their contact information if they don't see the value behind doing so. Think about your USP. If your page doesn't clearly tell them why they should sign up, it's failing to deliver this. The value proposition can be woven through the other page elements, but make sure it's there.

Logical Flow

Make sure the flow of the page guides the reader from the headline to the call-to-action quickly and logically. Don't put roadblocks up that will prevent or distract them from completing the desired action.

Dig Into the Pain

Your visitor found your site because they need a specific answer to something that they think you provide. Dig into that pain, and make sure the elements on your page amplify that pain and make it the central focus of your visitor by providing a solution to their pain points. Bullet points are very effective for this.

Enhance the Pleasure

Make sure the site also emphasizes the benefit, or pleasure, that your product or service will offer. Balance the pain points with the benefit you provide to see a greater number of conversions.

Testimonials

Having testimonials is a must. Why should people trust you? Always provide testimonials from satisfied customers who have seen their pain reduced with the use of your product or service. Remember customers say what you can't say about yourself without appearing as if you are bragging. Make sure the testimonials are from real people and include pictures and specifics. Again, video testimonials are the best, although text with a first name and last initial are acceptable. If no image is provided, ask permission to use their Facebook or LinkedIn picture as it adds credibility.

The testimonials need to be carefully selected and promoted to be effective. WikiJob learned this when they had three testimonials on the bottom of their homepage that weren't connected to a specific customer and were not highlighted as testimonials, but just looked like quotes. WikiJob did A/B testing and moved the testimonials to the top of the page, and they saw an increase in conversions of 34%. When people see that others had success working with you, they will be more willing to trust that you can help them as well. It's a powerful social influencer.

Easy to Contact

Provide your address, phone number, email, and any other contact methods on your landing page to assure site visitors that you're a real company or person, so they're more likely to provide their information. If you choose to add a live chat feature, make sure it's responsive and helpful. Also, include a navigation bar across the bottom of each page with links to your homepage, "About Us" page, and the Privacy Policy or Terms of Use. Google likes this, and it builds even more trust.

Powerful, Clear CTA

The call-to-action is the primary focus of your landing page. If people can't find it, your page will fail. Craft a CTA that's clear and powerful. It needs to be prominent, needs to explicitly tell the visitor what they're doing and needs to fit logically on the page, preferably above the fold (where they can understand the whole message in a five-second snapshot in a desktop or mobile view).

The Vineyard, a luxury hotel in London, learned the importance of the CTA. They had a CTA to "Book Hotel" at the bottom of their landing page that was just a link and was hard for visitors to find. By adding a new bright red button that was more prominent and higher on the page, they saw a 32.12% improvement in the number of bookings. It's not surprising that showing visitors what they're supposed to do improves your conversion rates. Help guide them.

Trust Triggers

Trust Triggers are items that create trust between the visitor and your company. Have you won awards? Has your work been cited in a news article? Perhaps you've been quoted on a popular blog? Part of the BBB maybe? These types of citations can help build the trust you need to get conversions. Don't forget about your safe site logos and secure checkout logos, which are essential if you're collecting payment from a potential buyer.

Valuable Lead Magnet

Make sure you have a substantial offer. If you have created a lead magnet, be sure it is valuable and something for which your prospects would be willing to pay. A lead magnet is an offer that you give to your subscribers or customers to convince them to give up their personal information, so it deserves a closer look. Use an image to show prospects what they will receive.

Lead Magnets – Fishing With the Right Lures

A lead magnet is a shiny object that you will give to your visitor in exchange for the personal information they provide. It's an essential component of the landing page because no one wants to provide their email or phone number for no reason. You have to hook them with the right bait to get their information.

Hesel Solicitors, who specializes in wills and probates, found this to be true. With seven local competitors offering the same basic packages, Hesel Solicitors had fierce competition. Also, wills and probates are not "sexy" products to sell, making them hard to market.

To stand out, Hesel Solicitors scripted a different conversation about why people need to write wills early in life. They ditched the wills and probate insider lingo, opting instead to create a message that reflected their target audience's everyday life. They also created a series of free videos that walked visitors through the steps to take before writing a will. This established trust, brought in a new audience and pushed Hesel Solicitors to the forefront of the market because of their friendly and helpful approach. As a result, their sales conversions increased from one out of every seven visitors to six out of every 10.

So what can you use as a bait? By now, you could probably put together this list on your own, but here is mine:

- *Free consultation* – Give a free consultation to new visitors to build the relationship (put a dollar value on your time).

- *Checklist, infographic, or guide* – Offer helpful information in an easy-to-digest format.

- *Surveys, quizzes, and assessments* – Let users test their knowledge or abilities or get feedback.

- *Reports and guides* – Offer expert insight into your topic that is exclusive to subscribers.

- *A coupon* – Everyone loves a deal; it's also best to include an expiration date to spur action.

- *Case studies and white papers* - Again, this gives the chance to position yourself as an expert and provide exclusive, helpful information.

- *Mini-courses* – Video or article-based courses are valuable because they're typically something for which you'd have to pay.

- *E-book* – An e-book is like a lengthy article with images and graphics, and it can be quite helpful to your customer. Make sure it is top-tier content.

As you can see, quite a bit of thought should go into creating a landing page. Though they appear simple, to be effective, they need to be carefully planned. With these tips and strategies, you should be well equipped to create effective landing pages for your websites, converting your site visitors into leads at a much higher rate through the power of landing pages.

Up to this point we have talked about manual things you need to do to create authority online. Next, let me show you how to grow your influence and scale your business quickly through paid ads and automation.

Getting More Traffic to Amplify Your Status

Clicks on paid search listings beat out organic clicks by nearly a 2:1 margin for keywords with high commercial intent. In other words, 64.6% of people click on Google Ads when they are looking to buy an item online!

– Larry Kim, founder of WordStream

I hear a lot about "organic" these days. Organic traffic. Organic reach. Organic results. Organic links. Organic produce. Just kidding...that last one has no bearing on our purpose here today. But the others? They absolutely do, and not for the better. I want to discuss the myth that organic traffic is the only kind worth having. I know we have already talked about several methods to get exposure organically, which all have a place in a well-rounded strategy, but have you seen the first page of Google these days? It's almost all ads!

So STOP overlooking the incredible potential of *paid* traffic!

What is Paid Traffic?

The goal of any type of traffic is to drive people to your website, where they can form a relationship with you and hopefully become a client or customer.

The money spent generating traffic to your site can be divided into two main categories: paid search (e.g., Google) and paid social (e.g., Facebook).

Benefits of Paid Traffic

Paid traffic is valuable in many ways. These include:

- It's faster than SEO – instantly on the first page of search results instead of waiting months for Google to rank your site organically
- You can control the traffic and turn it on or off at any time, and regulate how much traffic you receive
- Paid ads target people who are most likely to pay for your products and services
- Easy testing and quantifying your results
- You can jump to the top of everyone's newsfeeds
- You can target customer's likes, demographics, and behaviors
- Geo-target to reach only customers in your area
- Fast, easy way to test best marketing copy

As you can see, paid traffic carries with it significant benefits. It's amazing how many people forget this and think that only organic matters, and that if you can't generate traffic organically, then you're a failure.

Here's the truth: many, if not most, new businesses *can't* effectively generate organic traffic. Good SEO is very time-consuming, and therefore, expensive. Search results and social channels are saturated, and often, the local business landscape is as well. There are people who *want* what you sell, but if you can't find them, it doesn't matter much.

Now, before I continue, there is one caveat. I firmly believe that paid traffic is worth the money. However, you do have to track it carefully and watch Google. I have not bought into the Machine Learning that Google offers yet, where everything is automated. It's easy to get sucked into the trap of the "only pay when they click" mantra that Google promotes. Don't get confused! Google is out for your money! I would suggest never using AdWords Express and make sure to set up goals (i.e., phone calls, form submissions, downloads, purchases, and any other micro goals you think would be helpful to know).

Also, set up your Google Analytics account if you haven't already. If you are at all unsure about how to do this, I would highly recommend that you spend a little money and have someone that knows AdWords to at least set up your analytics, goals, and campaign structure or you will be wasting a lot of money on unwanted clicks. You need to have visibility into your campaign.

In the SEO Podcast, we always say, "Never throw money against the wall to see if it sticks. Test and measure. Always."

Here I feel like I should be providing you with some education on Customer Acquisition Cost, Lifetime Value, CTR, Relevancy Score, Keyword ROI, etc. Also, I feel I should explain how to set up a campaign as well as best practices I use, but I would not be doing you justice, I feel like a lot of this I would be better at showing you through a live training session or YouTube video where you can see my screen. I am a Google Partner and manage about $162,000+ in AdWords ad spend per month. I have read many books written about this topic, so hear me when I say this: One of the best I have ever read and would recommend is *Ultimate Guide to Google Adwords Fifth Edition* by Perry Marshall, Mike Rhodes, and Bryan Todd. For now, let me just stick to the "Why" and I will let Perry Marshall focus on the "How."

Why You Need Paid Search

Okay, so you're convinced paid traffic has a place in the world, but is it right for *you?* Good question. Let me say that I think, along with Perry Marshall, it's the best invention for small business marketing since the Internet!

Google receives around 3.5 billion searches per day. Every one of those searches represents a need, desire, or request for information. If you can scratch the itch of a tiny fraction of those people, you'll have a never-ending stream of leads and customers.

A quick case study will help us see the benefits for a small, local business. Consider Bedford Accountants that started late in 2016. They knew they had to meet tight deadlines if they wanted to be ready to go at the beginning of 2017, which is when lots of customers need self-assessments and is, therefore, the busiest time of year in the industry. They set up a well thought out AdWords campaign and went live in January 2017. They ended up generating leads for $21 apiece (Level Up Marketing, n.d.).

Considering the value of each client, this is a *very* inexpensive lead source. Also, if you take into account that they were a new business without much word-of-mouth marketing to draw on and very little content up online, those leads become doubly valuable. Could they have waited for organic results? Sure, but many businesses run in the red the first few years, and had they waited, they might not have made it.

Even if you're solidly in the black, who wants to just sit around and *wait?*

No one. Why not skip to the front of the line?

When a prospect types in a specific keyword, it serves up both organic search results *and* paid results. If you don't have a hope of appearing in the former, you can do much to grow your business by ensuring you show up in the latter. I love paid ads!

Finding Profitable Keywords

Keywords Research is a concept that takes only a moment to understand and a lifetime to master. A keyword is a word or phrase for which a prospect is already searching. When they type it in, Google trolls through organic and paid results and returns the ones that the algorithm deems most relevant to the search.

(This is true for Yahoo! and Bing as well, by the way, though neither of those platforms even combined are nearly as popular nor as profitable as Google. As of today, Google has about 74% of the search market.)

Your job is to figure out which keywords someone might be searching that would bring them to your business. Keywords may be very basic, such as "virtual assistant." The problem with that is, if that's the keyword you shoot for, you're likely to be buried under other, more qualified results.

That's why, typically, you want to focus on "intent" and shoot for long-tail phrases which are three and four keyword phrases that are very specific to the product or service you are selling.

Luckily, Google offers an easy-to-use keyword planning tool that will help you easily find these words and phrases. Using it takes practice, and know that it only shows you the paid results (not organic search), so it might be misleading depending on the data you are looking for, but take some time and play around with it. Other research tools I use are SEMRush, Moz's Keyword Explorer, and Spyfu.

Optimizing for Local Search

If you serve the local community, tailor your keywords to people in your area. Local search operates on the same basic keyword principles but is more targeted.

For instance, when someone types in "cat grooming Houston" on Google, and you *offer* cat grooming in Houston, you want to be on that list, right? Do you see how the word "Houston" provides more intent on what they are looking for? The prospect likely isn't searching to learn more about cat grooming, but instead is looking for a place that does cat grooming in Houston.

A significant amount of science, research, behavior analysis and experience go into most campaigns. You have to optimize for local in most campaigns to maximize the effectiveness of your ad dollars to win the right bids and get conversions.

For more on the basics of how to set up a campaign, check out: BuildYourBrandMania.com/Resources.

Paid Social and Why You Need It

Paid social, as the name suggests, is traffic generated through social media sites, mainly Facebook. Advertising on social media isn't new, and it is currently very affordable, but a surprising number of people don't take advantage of it. I don't think that businesses as a whole have realized that social media has revolutionized the way we can advertise. People now have a way to interact with brands, ads, and companies, which opens up a whole new level of marketing opportunities. Engagement allows you to develop a relationship with your prospects as they go through the customer journey like never before. Customer service has also taken on a new meaning. If you are unhappy about something, you can tweet at the company about it and see how quickly most brands respond!

Case Study – Stine Home & Yard

Let's look at a case study involving Louisiana-based home improvement store Stine Home & Yard on how social can directly impact a business's sales. Generally, people don't search for and buy these products on the internet because they can go to a nearby store to shop. Stine had spent a lot of money on TV and local print ads in the past and was looking for a less expensive way to promote special deals and events to drive in-store sales.

Stine used Facebook ads to promote seasonal events such as "Labor Day Tax-Free Weekend." Photos of customers with sales signs, images from the company's coupon book, and promotional videos were targeted to people living within 50 miles of the Louisiana store. Additional promotions were offered through Facebook ads, and exclusive deals and contests were offered in Stine Home & Yards Facebook group. In a 12-month period, Stine's sales increased more than 10% while advertising costs decreased by 22%.

The success was based on a number of factors common to Facebook Ads:

1. Fine-tuned targeting
2. A large mobile audience
3. Facebook Insights (analytics)
4. Increased brand awareness
5. Upward trending click-through rates

If you can combine a range of ad types with local relevance and intelligent incentivizing, you too can put social to work for you and your business.

Setting up a Facebook Ads account can be overwhelming. You must have a personal page, which you need to use to create your business page. There is a Business Account and an Ads account. The Business Account can make changes to the page but cannot create or change ads. The Ads account can make ads but cannot make updates or changes to the news feed. You control access to these with the Business Manager account.

Once you get it going, you can try out the new "lead form" option. You will love it, especially if you don't have a strong landing page or if you are sending traffic directly to your website. Most websites are not set up to capture leads; they are meant to be digital brochures.

Understanding Your Ad's Intent

Here's a brief breakdown:

Brand Awareness – These campaigns are geared toward ensuring people know who you are. They let customers know what you can do and how you can help them, and direct visitors to where they can find out more.

Store Visits – This type of ad helps you drive people to a store, whether it's online or local. If you have a local store, you must set up a locations structure on your business page.

Local Awareness – This is similar to the Brand Awareness ad type except that it focuses on a very specific geographic area. Instead of a picture, you can use video to drive even more engagement.

Clicks to Website – This is the best approach to get visitors to a page to take a specific action or only consume your content. You can use a rotating carousel of images to send them to different links, although we have had mixed results with carousels; usually, they work better though. You can also tag visitors that visit a particular page and create a custom list to show them ads later.

Event – Advertising a big upcoming event? Create the right kind of hype with these ads, which let you enhance your other ad efforts. If you want people to RSVP on your site, however, it may be better to drive them to your site first using a Website Conversions ad.

Lead Generation – These take people directly to a landing page. The visitor is already primed to take action, so make sure there is action to take: sign up for a newsletter, download a free offer, start a free trial, or even make a purchase. If possible, allow visitors only to be able to take *one* action. Make sure your offer is something your prospects will value enough to be willing to exchange their contact information for it.

Page Likes – Sometimes you just want more likes to give a new Facebook business page more social proof and encourage others to check out what you have going on.

Post Engagement – Similarly, sometimes you want people to interact with your posts. Encourage visitors to comment, or provide a survey, to elicit feedback on your products or services.

That said, let's focus on a particular ad sequence that will leverage your new "Trusted Advisor Status" and have prospects coming to you regularly.

Leveraging My 3-Step Trusted Advisor Method

If you're looking to unlock the power of Facebook in your marketing, I would recommend what I call a Facebook "Trusted Advisor Campaign," which is a three-step advertising strategy that involves three separate campaigns:

1. **Educate:** Generate awareness and consideration for your business by providing free value, perhaps by helping prospects understand a complex subject or offering DIY tutorials to establish yourself as an expert.

2. **Engage:** Engage your audience through Surveys, Contests, Opinion Questions and more to start building a relationship with them.

3. **Convert:** Promote your services and encourage prospects to pull the trigger with time-sensitive offers after you have delivered multiple views and created some brand recall by watching your frequency and relevancy scores.

"Wait," you're wondering, "Why can't I just skip to step three and tell them how great I am?"

Good question, and to answer that with a relatively simple answer: because people don't come to Facebook to buy products and services. They come to interact with friends, to comment on the "state of the union," to share their latest smoothie recipes, and track their favorite gurus. Think cocktail party, not shopping mall. People often use Facebook to get away from having to make decisions. Going to Facebook to buy items is not how people currently use the platform – at least, not yet.

That's why you need to use a campaign strategy that begins with making the prospect aware of your brand and educating them on how you could help. Then perhaps they will visit your Facebook business page, visit your website, read your blog, and so on, at which point they may be ready to buy. They won't be prepared to buy the first time they see your ad on Facebook, so at first, your ads need to take a different form.

Your awareness ads can be curated posts, informing them of how to do something – plan a great vacation, measure serving sizes, whatever. Your ads must establish that you know what you're talking about and that the prospect needs your help. Again, though, they are informational.

Engage your audience to build rapport. I like to see about 35% engagement with my organic posts and a decent level of engagement and frequency with my ads before making a pitch to a new audience. Check out Facebook Insights if you haven't done so yet. There is a ton of great data there that can help you better target your audience and tailor your message.

Only then is it time to make your pitch, with a URL or phone number (or another contact medium), as well as a clear call to action. It's a marathon, not a sprint. You have to commit to a long-term strategy on Facebook to really see solid results.

Remarketing: Your Secret Weapon

Did you know that 96% of people leave a website without making a purchase, filling out a lead form, or making a social share? Instead, people visit a website, and then they check out competitors, price shop, or get distracted and start watching cat videos on YouTube.

Has this ever happened to you?

You visit a site and then begin to see that company advertised everywhere, from Facebook to Google search, to the various web pages you visit throughout the day. Amazon is superb at this. While it might seem like the universe is conspiring to get you to buy a particular product, in fact, you're just being remarketed or retargeted.

You might not recognize the term "remarketing," but you know what it is. According to Search Engine Journal, "Remarketing, also known as retargeting, are banner ads that target you after you've visited a company's website."

(Kilbourn, 2014) These ads can boost ad response rates up to 400%, and nearly three out of five online buyers said they noticed ads for products they viewed on other sites says Wishpond (wishpond, n.d.).

Remarketing involves a small snippet of code that you embed into your site, which doesn't affect the performance of the site at all except to tag your visitor like a laser-guided missile, marking that they have visited your page. This creates a custom audience to which you can later show messages. Remarketing can tell a story if you create a sequence of different messages in a particular order using offers, USP's, and maybe testimonials or case study data. It's similar to an email marketing sequence, but without the email!

Why You Should Use Remarketing

The primary benefit of remarketing is that it exposes your targeted visitors to your brand over and over again improving brand awareness as well as increasing your conversion rates. Retargeted visitors are four times more likely to convert than new visitors. You can then improve the relevance of the ads based on their behaviors. Typically, it takes many different touches to get a customer to buy something, and remarketing does that in a cost-effective way. After seeing your brand and being sent to your site repeatedly, they are much more likely to pull the trigger on your product or service. You will feel familiar to them, and that increases the chance they will pick you over your competitors.

Simply put, you should use it because your customers have already proven they're more likely to be interested in your product or service. So, spending ad dollars on remarketing is more likely to result in a higher ROI for your ads.

Case Study – Loews Hotel Group

Loews Hotel Group shifted 70% of their offline ad spend to online. Loews used Contextual Targeting and Retargeting on Google's Display Network. Revenue increased 10%, bookings were up 9%, and there was a 5% increase in unique site visitors. The $800 remarketing campaign produced $60,000 in sales! (think with Google, 2013)

Great! Where Can I Set Up a Campaign?

In addition to Google AdWords, you can set up campaigns with AdRoll, which enables you to easily reach Facebook, Google, Yahoo, and Microsoft ad platforms. It's a one-stop shop that makes it easy to cover all your bases. You can also use Perfect Audience, which is straightforward to use and compatible with a wide range of sites. I like it.

As you can see, there exists a wealth of approaches to generating paid traffic. Each form brings you the same benefits that organic traffic does. It's surprising how few people leverage paid traffic, perhaps thinking that paying for traffic somehow decreases their legitimacy or maybe because they don't know how it works.

How to Create a Solid Ad

Use Relevant Keywords or Themes – If you are using keyword-based retargeting, consistency between the search phrase and the keywords displayed in the ads that appear in the results is important. If the retargeting is display-based, it's essential to use themes that will resonate with buyers. Use the word they might be searching for in your ad.

Focus on Customer Benefits – Remember that it is never about you; it's about the benefits your product or services provide or solves for them. Create ads geared toward your customer's specific wants or desires. Typically they are looking for a solution to a problem.

Try Various Offers – Use different offers in your ads and see what works best. Give them a reason to pick you. For example, "Buy One, Get One 1/2 Off," or "Get a bonus with this purchase." I am also a big fan of value adds and not giving discounts. Discounts devalue your product or service, so try to avoid them whenever possible.

Try Limited Time Offers – These create a sense of urgency and push people to act fast.

Include Specific Calls To Action – Make sure you know what you want the outcome to be and gear the ad toward that goal. Use phrases such as "Buy Now," "For a Limited Time," "Sign Up Today," "Download Free Report," etc.

Use Compelling Images – Images are attributed to 70-75% of the success of a display ad. They are by far the number one reason people are attracted to ads. Also, Google and Facebook typically only give you 20% of the ad space for words, so your images need to communicate what you are offering. Show the product you are offering!

Create Strong Headlines – In remarketing, you can be more creative with your headlines and get people to click out of curiosity so make them count.

You should continuously be A/B Testing one ad versus another to see how they perform. Test the frequency or cadence along with the time of day, bid adjustments and audiences to which you are marketing. That is the great thing about digital advertising vs. traditional media – you can see the data in real time and course-correct your ads, messaging, and offers. Remember all the stuff we talk about regarding landing pages because ads and landing pages go hand in hand.

More Remarketing Fire Power

You can remarket or retarget visitors that leave your site in various ways, not just in the Google display network with banner ads. (I am not going to go into CPV/PPV Networks here as there are too many caveats) Here's a summary of some of the other weapons in your retargeting arsenal:

Remarketing Lists for Search Ads (RLSA) – RLSA allows you to customize the campaign for your search ads to new and previous visitors to your site. You can tailor your bids and ads to these visitors when they're searching on Google or Bing. This is great to be able to segment your ad dollars to "zero in" on a particular audience. Bing remarketing also extends to shopping. If you are not using Bing, you are missing out.

Social Retargeting – Social retargeting refers to marketing to people based on their social actions and interactions. For example, targeting people who like your company's Facebook page, follow you on Twitter, or people that have visited your website is a good strategy. I recommend everyone with a website set up a Facebook Pixel and a retargeting campaign, at a minimum. It will only cost you a few dollars per month and will significantly reduce your customer acquisition cost. It is surprising to me how many businesses don't do this.

Email Retargeting – Email retargeting is a powerful tool you can use to follow up with people if they have opened an email, clicked on a link, or watched a video in the email, etc. This gets pretty advanced with if/then logic, and if you're at a place where you are already doing some email marketing, and you want to increase the sophistication in your responses, I would recommend using Active Campaign, Ontraport, or Hubspot. AWeber and MailChimp can only go so far, at the moment.

Hopefully, this chapter taught you some ways to bring qualified prospects to your door, build trust, and move them into your sales process. Paid traffic brings you the some of the same benefits that organic traffic does with one crucial difference: a lot more of it is available to you RIGHT NOW, it is scalable, and you don't have to wait to reach your target audience months down the road. I encourage you to utilize paid traffic if you haven't started already.

The Fortune is in the Follow-Up

Did you know that around 80% of sales are made on the 5th to 12th contact a company has with a customer? Did you know that most salespeople stop at three?

A lot of communication must be made to gain a sale. Luckily, email marketing has made it much easier as well as more affordable to reach out, make contact, and stay in touch. As a salesman-turned-marketer, this was a game changer. I can do what ten – maybe even 20 – salespeople could do by automating parts of my sales process.

Email marketing, like any other type of marketing, can be a positive or a negative experience for the recipient. The spam messages you'll find in your junk mail folder selling foreign pharmaceuticals are the worst of the worst. The best email marketing messages give you information about a product or company you'd like to try, delivered in a way that makes it seem natural and like someone is looking out for you. People don't like HTML templates that look like ads as soon as you open them. Simple text emails tend to work the best.

Consider the following benefits of email marketing:

Build Brand Awareness – When you send marketing emails, consumers gain additional exposure to your business, brand, and name. You build long-term value for your brand with every message you send as it helps you stay in touch with your audience.

Sharing is Simple – Because you take the time to create accessible, useful and interesting email content, you may gain additional traction because some of your subscribers will forward or share the message to associates in their niche and that will build your influence.

The Analytics Don't Lie – You will be able to track your results because email marketing is inherently measurable. The analytics associated with sending messages are an indispensable tool for you to measure the success of your campaign and decide what to do with it in the future.

It's Cost-Effective – The low cost of entry and the high return-on-investment make email marketing one of the most affordable ways to get the word out to new and returning customers alike.

Did you know that most people keep their email address for ten or more years? Now that's dedication. This is just one reason it pays to stick with a tried and true method of customer outreach.

Is Email Marketing Still Relevant?

Many business owners wonder if email marketing is still relevant and regardless whether they believe it or not, most small business owners do not do it. This is a HUGE opportunity for those that are smart enough to see it and invest the time and money to do it right. Why? Well, for starters consider the numbers. According to Radici.com, 3.7 billion people around the world utilize email (Anton, 2018). Even as social media websites and other forms of online contact grow and change, email has remained stable and is accessed by a high percentage of users.

Even if a social media platform grows and becomes huge today, it could become irrelevant tomorrow – think MySpace, for instance. Plus, popular websites and social channels in one country may be but a blip on the radar in others. I'm also not saying that paid social doesn't have a place. I love paid social, but email is likely to continue to be an essential form of contact, especially in the business world, where flashy isn't always effective.

It all comes down to getting your message seen. Compare email marketing to social media marketing, and you will notice one thing: email marketing wins hands down. On average, one out of five marketing emails is opened, out of the opens they typically get a click-through rate of 3.57%. However, on Facebook, you will usually see a click-through rate of only 0.07% (Zhel, 2016). An email inbox is a virtual home address for someone that you can directly send mail to year after year.

Case Study: DocketFish's Email Marketing

DocketFish is a service designed to make legal document and docket retrieval cheaper and more efficient. DocketFish was popular among beta testers, and many of those users went on to become the startup's first customers. While the creators knew they had a great product, they wanted to make sure they stayed connected with their prospects. They went all out in their email marketing efforts, and within just a few weeks they saw a substantial increase in their customer base. Utilizing this approach can help grow the customer base of nearly any business with a strong interest base already in place.

The Spam Factor

Another concern that some business owners may have regarding email and email marketing is the spam factor. After all, there is a fine line between a promotional message and what could be construed as spam. Not only is spam annoying to your potential customers, but if you are not careful, it can also lead to legal issues for you.

The solution is straightforward: take proper precautions to make sure that your promotional messages are not spam. Don't use words like free, buy, or cash, as these trigger spam filters. If you are doing everything you can to assure that your message is beneficial to your customer and not an annoyance, chances are you're covered. The key is to present a message that is valuable to the reader. If it is not, you're not doing your job as a marketer. Here are some tips to help assure your marketing messages are not perceived as spam.

Make it Easy to Unsubscribe – One of the easiest ways you can avoid spam-like marketing is to make it easy for recipients to unsubscribe from your mailing list. Place the unsubscribe link at the top or bottom of your messages and don't try to hide it.

Segment – By segmenting your marketing message you accomplish two things. First and foremost, you assure that the content you send is relevant to the receiver. Second, you reduce the number of messages a consumer receives making it feel less like spam.

Fulfill Your Promises – The number one way that you can reduce spam complaints is to fulfill the promise that you made to the customer when they signed up for your email list. If you promised sales and discounts, then deliver sales and discounts. If you promised a video course, deliver high-quality videos packaged with loads of value. Go the extra mile to offer something unique to email recipients ONLY so they feel that it is worth it to get your messages.

Note: If you are emailing people from a list that did not double opt-in or you have not emailed in a while, scrub your list with free software like *Bulk Email Checker* or *Hunter.io* to ensure the emails are still valid.

Emails get a bad rap because some marketers have gone overboard with "Cold Email Marketing" and go long periods of time between sending messages. You should increase the frequency at which you send messages. Yes, you read that right. Most people think if they send an email monthly, weekly, or daily they are "bothering people;" this is a fallacy. If you are sending high-quality content that the reader wants, then actually the opposite is true. Sending emails sporadically or only every three months will likely cause your message to be marked as SPAM as recipients may forget who you are or that they even subscribed to your list. Remember you are building relationships. Who do you have a close relationship with that you only talk to every three to six months? Or worse that you only reach out to when you want something? I think you get my point.

Let's take a step back and describe how to get your emails opened.

5 Rules to Make Sure Your Emails Get Opened

Why do you send customers or potential customers email marketing messages? Chances are you're hoping to build a relationship or build your authority with value, or maybe to get the word out about a new product or service. The only way to accomplish this is if the message is welcomed, opened, and read by the recipient. "Permission Based Marketing". There is more to consider when it comes to getting your message opened than you may have realized.

RULE 1: Personalize It

Trusted advisors can provide more personalized experiences with their marketing campaigns, and email marketing is no exception. An email message with a customized subject line is more likely to be opened than one without – and that's just the beginning. Personalizing your email marketing is the first step in creating a message that appears welcoming and beneficial to the recipient.

Personalization includes referring to the recipient by name or another identifying factor (such as birth date or job title) to get open rates similar to an email from someone they might know well.

RULE 2: Use a Compelling Subject Line

A compelling subject line is probably the most important way that you can get your email message opened. Spend some time looking at the messages you receive every day and think about the ones that you open. This is where I spend a lot of time when crafting an email because if your email is never opened, your message is never heard.

You are also more likely to open an email if it either refers to something that interests you or if it seems as though it may be from a friend or loved one rather than from a big faceless corporation. My favorite subject line is "checking in."

Case study: During Barack Obama's presidential campaign, his marketing team collected the email addresses of potential voters. Voters who had shared their email address with the campaign started receiving messages from Barack Obama with intriguing subject lines such as "Join me for dinner?", "Wow", "It doesn't have to be this way" and other similar titles. According to Toby Fallsgraff, director of his campaign, "The subject lines that worked best were things you might see in your inbox from other people. 'Hey' was probably the best one we had over the duration." (Ouimet, 2013) By taking the time to create a compelling subject line, you will likely put your message in front of many more readers. While these may seem odd, they worked.

RULE 3: Utilize the Preheader

The email preheader is the text that appears either below or next to the subject line in both mobile and desktop email platforms. Without even realizing it, many people "hover" over a message before deciding to click it or delete it. This preheader text offers you the chance to reel in your prospect. Using these few words you can develop enough interest that the recipient feels compelled to click on the message and see what else you have to say. Some best practices for this preheader space are:

Build on What the Subject Line States – Don't repeat the subject line or provide entirely new information. Instead, build on what the subject line teases. You want your recipient to be curious about what's beneath the fold.

Think About the Breaks – When you can create a cliffhanger by breaking off the header where the reader will want more information, you are going to boost your open rates.

Make it Irresistible – The preheader is the space where you'll want to promote any out-of-this-world deals you are highlighting. Make sure that the reader will have to click to get the majority of the information. Using your preheader to create a sense of urgency is always a good idea.

RULE 4: Be Mobile-Ready

More people than ever use mobile devices to access email, not only in the consumer world but also for B2B. So, there is no excuse for sending a marketing message that isn't mobile-friendly. Follow industry best practices, but also test it yourself by viewing the message on multiple devices.

You can use a service like EmailOnAcid.com to see how your email will appear on the most popular phones, clients, apps, and devices, but most email autoresponders like

MailChimp or AWeber do a pretty good job, I would always check with a test email if you can.

RULE 5: Segment Your List

As part of the personalization aspect of your email marketing campaign, you should sit down and give your email list a good hard look. Put time and effort into building the best list possible. However, this is a full book in itself. Jeff Walker's Launch lessons are a great place to begin. It boils down to building not just a big list, but a successful one. I recommend "Product Launch Formula" by Jeff Walker; it's a great read that will explain this stuff in more detail.

Then it comes time to segment your list. What is BEST way to do this?

Ask for their preference. One way to segment or group your contacts is by using email lists and asking your subscribers to specify what topics in which they are interested. Even if you don't understand segmenting, this concept should be crystal clear–you're getting customers signed up for information that is only valuable to them. People will fall into different buckets based on their personas, their engagement, and where they fall in the sales cycle.

Pay attention to purchasing behavior. Determine what your audience is interested in by using your email reports to see which messages they open and which links they click on. Add those people to an existing list or create a new one. You can also create lists for customers who purchased a particular product or service and send them emails. Remind them that they made a good decision purchasing from you and educate them on other services or products you offer in which they might be interested. It is called a "bump" when you present a higher value/cost offer right after something of low value is purchased. Bumps are typically done from a landing page, but I have also seen some success through a sequenced email format.

Focus on your relationship. Segment by the relationship or customer status to get the right information in front of the right people. You may send a different message or series of messages to new email signups than you send to former customers or someone who signed up months ago but has never acted.

Consider this example of Oak Furniture Land (Baldwin, 2015). Oak Furniture Land used email marketing to connect its 62 physical stores and its online presence to consumers who may have only shopped in a physical store or who may have only shopped online. The marketing team collected postcode information from customers who signed up for emails and used the information to geo-target a pre-Christmas email campaign. By doing this, the company could share messages that related directly to a customer's local store. The result? **A 40% increase in email-generated revenue.** The lesson to you is that the more relevant a message, the more likely it is to inspire customers to take action.

One final way to look at segmenting is to realize that different customers have a different value to you. A repeat customer will pay off more than someone who blindly signed up for an email list yesterday. Your goal should be to turn everyone into a raving fan, but in the meantime, each customer type needs different strategies to assure success. You need to have separate lists for different objectives and different audiences.

Writing Infotainment to Engage and Persuade

When you get an email subscriber to click on the message and read what's inside, you don't want to disappoint. The majority of email marketers make one of two mistakes:

1. Giving away too much content without doing enough selling
2. Selling too much without giving away enough content

Remember, your goal is to write emails in a way that will satisfy the reader's desire for useful information and content while also persuading them to buy or otherwise take action. If you do it correctly, the recipients will not feel as though you are trying to sell to them. No one likes to be sold to, but people love to buy! Think of what you're doing as professionally helping someone buy. They will view you as a trusted advisor and be happy to take your advice.

Inject Personality

The simplest way to engage your customers while being persuasive is to inject YOUR personality into your email content. Instead of trying to sell someone on a product or service using cold hard facts, which certainly have their place, appeal to the reader by showing the human personality behind the product.

Connect with their emotions. Don't be afraid to be funny, sarcastic, or sentimental - whatever suits the mood of your pitch and you. Rise above boring, pitch-filled nonsense, and you'll keep your readers in for the long haul. Build a relationship with them.

A well-known business rule states that 80% of your results come from 20% of your efforts. Perry Marshall explains this concept in depth in his book *80/20 Sales & Marketing*. Realizing the importance of this rule will help you get more results from less work, by adding a touch of personality. Besides, if they don't like you, why would you want to do business with them anyway?

Tell Stories

Use the storytelling skills we discussed. Remember, people love stories. Since childhood, we've been conditioned to enjoy sitting back and watching, reading, or listening to a story with a beginning, middle, and an end. Utilize this pattern to keep readers engaged and excited to read what you have to say next.

If you are still having trouble, let me introduce one more concept that can be used in not only emails but in all storytelling. Use the Pixar method. All of their movies follow this general plotline and have been successful. Think *Finding Nemo*.

1. Once upon a time...
2. Every day...
3. One day...

4. Because of that...

5. Until finally...

Another story that has impacted sales and captured people's emotions is TOMS shoes. For each pair of shoes sold by the company, they donate a pair of shoes. To date, TOMS has given over 60 million pairs of shoes to kids who need them most. This is a great reason why a consumer may want to shop TOMS. Infotainment can bring that stat to life using stories. TOMS shares stories about individuals and groups who've received these shoes and show what a significant impact they have had. These stories turn something intangible into something that can be felt and appreciated. Remember, emails can be one long story that you drip to your prospects one piece at a time.

Pop Culture References

Pop culture references may be frowned upon in many types of content writing. However, when sending an email, they are suddenly quite effective. It is easy to reference something that is current and on the minds of people today. The benefit is that since it is an email message, you don't have to worry about it becoming stale or outdated before the consumer reads it. Pop culture references can help connect your brand with the world at large. Using something current always drives up engagement.

Be Brief

Remember the digital attention span is quite short, so it's important to be brief while getting your message across. Don't let your email message become too wordy or you're likely to lose readers along the way. Have one message you are trying to communicate in each email. Focus on the benefits of whatever it is you are selling and make them transparent. Don't lose sight of your specific goal while you strive to connect with readers.

Convert Subscribers to Clients with the Call to Action

If your marketing email has been successful to this point, this might be the 11th hour, and you now have the opportunity to turn that subscriber into a client. This is where the call to action comes into place.

If your call to action isn't successful and clear, then your email campaign is not going to perform well. I think I have driven this point home, but here are the basics.

K.I.S.S. – Keep it Simple, Stu*id

Choose ONE distinct call to action per message. If you offer too many options for the reader to do, you risk overwhelming and confusing them. At the same time, make sure you include at least one call to action above the fold or above the first scroll to make sure it is noticed by someone quickly skimming your email.

Action Words

The call to ACTION is called that for a reason, "Do this now!" Make sure you inspire action by utilizing action words or verbs as a driver to your message. If you want to test beyond the basics, try using *Roget's Descriptive Word Finder* or *Roget's Thesaurus*.

Your call to action doesn't have to be dull, boring, or like everyone else's. When you can make this message stand out, you'll be more likely to reach subscribers who are tired of the same old thing.

Pro Tip: Make sure you don't lose your call to action in an image. While images can have an impact on email marketing, they are sometimes not included (especially for mobile views) due to load time and other factors. So, make sure your CTA is text as well, or it could get lost if you embed it in an image.

Use the What, Why, How Rule

When building your call to action, a simple rule to follow is the "What, Why, How" rule. You want to tell people what to do, why they should do it, and how to do it. In its simplest form, it could be "Click Here" to save big on your next "widget purchase" by shopping with us. The *What* is "Click Here," the *Why* is "to save big," and the *How* is "by shopping with us." Make sure it's personalized to the user.

Wondering how important this simple call to action is? 90% of visitors who read a headline will read the call to action, too! If you hook them, you can reel them in, also. Happy fishing!

Automate It

"Automate, Delegate, or Eliminate."

– Aaron Weathers
Lead Generation Specialist @eWebResults

While you'll spend plenty of hands-on time working on your email marketing campaign, you can't possibly do everything by hand if you want to make a significant impact.

Automation is key to the success of a modern marketing program. Essentially, an automation email program sends messages for you once you've input some basic information. A little work up front and it will pay off time and time again.

Let me break down what makes automation successful and easy. Keep in mind, this is just the surface, as there are entire books written about this topic. I also want to stress that emails should not wholly replace phone calls. Conversation is what creates customers; automation creates leverage.

I'd like to give a quick shout-out to Robert Neumann for all that he has taught me on this subject.

Okay, let's get started:

Choose a Goal – Determine what you're trying to accomplish and make sure you keep this in mind throughout every step of automation. Are you trying to get a new client, convince an existing customer to buy again, or perhaps you just want to set up a consultation? Each of these goals will be written in a different tone and positioned differently.

Segment List – As we've discussed, segmenting is the first step towards personalization. Determine how it would be best to segment your subscriber list so you can create message groups that will receive personalized marketing content.

Choose the Right Software – There are many automation programs on the market. A number of them now incorporate SMS (text) which is extremely powerful. SMS open rates are what emails use to be: close to 99%! Research what each program does best and choose one that will help you reach your audience with as little work as possible. I am certified in Email Marketing with Hubspot, which gives me more inside knowledge about their offerings, which are fantastic albeit a little pricey. If you are a small business, MailChimp, Aweber, or Active Campaign are probably more than sufficient.

Map Out a Sequence – What tone are you going to open with: Quirky, Tease, or Techie? Also, think beyond the first message. How will the marketing sequence function? Will you be sending messages at set intervals, or to coincide with specific events? What are your behavior-based triggers? What will your cadence be? Think through all of this. I use Active Campaign, and they have many great features that you can manipulate if/then logic to anything you can think of that is easy to map out. Ontraport is a platform you can use to tie the emails to actions, other emails, and to your landing pages. This can become complex, but it does give you a much fuller view to map out the customer journey.

Lay Out Your Topics – Create an editorial calendar of what you would like to convey to your reader and how you want to build your relationship as if you could do this manually with each reader. I like to start with an offer, then a trust-building email, a testimonial, a quick reminder email, then back to an offer, and so on. I typically send emails on days one, two, four, and seven. Then I stagger them once a week for the rest of the month and check in once a month for up to six months. It just depends on the campaign you are running.

Writing the Emails – This is where it all happens. You can finally put all that studying to work and begin creating emails to go out to your subscribers. Just remember all you've learned so far and you will make a significant impact. Your email should be no longer than 150 words. You can use the Seinfeld Method here (another thing I learned from Russell Brunson). You can write a story about anything really – just be sure you tie it back to what you are communicating. Link it to a blog or a landing page to increase your relationship with the reader, Focus on one topic at a time.

Creating a successful email marketing campaign is both an art and a science. Realize that you may not experience the results you desire on your first go round. Practice makes perfect. Determine what works and what doesn't work and make changes. A/B Test. It boils down to just getting started. If your competition hasn't mastered email marketing yet, this could be your chance to pull ahead. And if you ARE using the techniques mentioned above, you have even more inspiration to avoid getting left behind!

Conclusion

First and foremost, I acknowledge that I have presented you with a *lot* of information in this book. You may be feeling a little overwhelmed by the massive "to do" list that's now scrolling through your head.

I want to assure you that you don't need to feel that way. Building a personal brand is not an overnight process, and becoming a recognized thought leader will take time. If you are comparing yourself to major successes in your niche – or other niches – you're bound to get discouraged. You simply can't compete out of the gate with those who have put years into their brands when you're just beginning to learn the basics.

So, don't try. You'll only drive yourself nuts.

Instead, make a list. I encourage you to take as many passes through this book as you need and write everything down that jumps out at you. While the book presents a fairly comprehensive road map and is structured in a way that gives you "to do" items that build naturally upon one another from beginning to end, you should reorder these tasks to fit your situation. Remember your Brand Mania starts and ends with *you!*

That said, it is essential to put in the time to get started right away. Now that you have a deeper understanding of what a personal brand is and how to build one that sticks, it's time to use the tools of success that are at your fingertips. Through dedicating time and effort to building your brand, you will slowly – and then quickly – rise above your competition and gain authority and recognition in your field.

This is the secret to online marketing in any industry. While advertisements, blog posts and S.M.A.R.T. social media campaigns all play a significant role, consistently building your personal brand is the No. 1 step you can take to achieve business success. In fact, until you truly understand this, you'll have a hard time realizing long-term results from any one of these strategies alone.

Now that you've read all the way through (or naughtily skipped to the end – that's right, I caught you), you understand how much more exists behind that tired promise of "Get to the front page of Google and your phone will ring off the hook!" You've seen it's not the whole story, and you now have a huge internet marketing toolkit or in Perry Marshall's words, "a Swiss army knife" to not only get you to the first page but to dominate your competition.

So, let's recap: You want more clients and customers. You want to be the "go to" person in your industry. Now whether you're a florist, wedding planner, lawyer, dentist, MLM professional or marketer yourself, the only thing that keeps a business going is bringing in *new* business. Attrition is an unfortunate fact of life, so you simply have to keep those leads flowing. But as we have seen throughout this book, a lead will not always become a customer, no matter how promising that lead looks.

You need to qualify those leads as real prospects and turn those prospects into customers before you get anywhere. But you didn't read this book because you need a lesson in the numbers game that is entrepreneurship or how to build a sales funnel or maybe you did? You're reading it because you understand – hopefully now more than ever – the importance of a personal brand and want the wisdom and know how to turn your expertise into a trusted source of information, products, and services for others.

From here, your job is to turn the personal branding strategies you have learned into a workable system for getting people to know, like, and trust you. Remember the story about tricky Mr. Frank Abagnale, who stood outside the bank at night with his "Out of Order" sign, convincing customers to give him their money? No one even questioned him. Instead, he got a courteous "Good night" or "Thank You."

What was his secret?

Simply this: He exploited the universal human tendency to place trust in people who look as though they deserve it. By putting on the uniform and standing next to a financial institution, he hijacked its credibility.

Good news is you are in an even better place than Mr. Abagnale because you have earned your expertise. If someone were to question you, you would likely know how to respond. You understand the ins and outs of your industry, and you could explain in clear terms why your prospects should work with you and what value they will get from so doing.

Most of the entrepreneurs and business owners with whom I consult already have a solid foundation of expertise and academic understanding of their fields. That's not the problem. The problem is that most lack confidence or don't know how to put themselves out there and get some PR and exposure. The problem can magnify when we consider the Edelman Trust Barometer, which says that strength of your professional reputation is even more important than the quality of your products and services. Simply put, you need *credibility* to sell.

Luckily, now you know the solution. If you can turn yourself into a Trusted Advisor who not only acts the part but outwardly looks the part, you will gain the confidence, exposure, and influence you need to start from a point of trust with your prospects, closing more deals and start on the path to building the business of your dreams.

Also remember to exude the values of communication, believability, relevancy, likeability, safety, and attractiveness. Only when you forge strong relationships through communication, prove yourself both believable and relevant to the prospect's needs, show yourself to be a safe bet, and present a good appearance will you generate the kind of business for which you're looking.

And only when you can clearly communicate your unique selling proposition, what makes you *you* and what makes you the most qualified to help *them*, will you succeed. Once again, that is founded upon the trifecta of:

1. Ethos: an appeal to ethics, used to convince someone of the credibility of the persuader
2. Pathos: an appeal to emotion, used to create a convincing emotional response
3. Logos: an appeal to logic and persuades the audience through reason

I urge you to not miss out on the authority that comes with personal branding. As I've discussed previously, we instinctively put our trust in authority. Anyone who has the backing of a large following, a degree, or a number of successes under their belt seems to appear to know what they are talking about automatically.

That's not to say you should fool people into thinking you know more than you do; I mean that if you want to convey that you *do* know what you're talking about, you need external or social proof – i.e., a personal brand to which people respond, and a message worth listening to.

Remember also that just one negative comment will wipe out roughly five to ten positive statements about your character and trustworthiness. That means you need to pay attention to what other people are saying about you. Set up those Google Alerts. If you don't know what it is others are saying online about you, searchers are only hearing one side of the story when they are looking for your services online, and your business could suffer.

Therefore, a key part of personal branding is to counteract any negative statements through reputation management. It is essential if you want to create buoyancy with more positive reviews while pushing down the negative results in search engines. Not only will this help you bring in new customers who trust you, but it will keep you in good standing with your existing clients and customers.

There is another reason not to wait before creating your personal brand. The longer you wait, the more time you give your competition to take these exact steps. Given a head start of enough years, and they may build a brand that outperforms your brand altogether that you will never be able to overcome.

Start today, and brand yourself proactively! Remember, branding is not about market share. It is about *mindshare*, creating a strong level of likability and trust between you and your prospects. You need to build a relationship with your target market that convinces them that they want to continue that relationship.

This approach works in any market, in any industry and at any time. As I've said, people connect with people, not with products or faceless companies. They will give you their business once they perceive you to be the best solution to their current problem or problems.

Recapping on how to turn yourself into that solution? By using information as your currency. I know through my experience working with many business owners that giving away free information can sometimes be painful. It feels as though you are divulging hard-earned secrets and giving people the information they need to solve their problems without ever compensating you.

Yet that is not the case if done systematically. What you are doing is giving away enough wisdom to help lead your prospects into clarifying their problems so that they become more aware of your solution. Once they have become your prospects, you can then market to them much more effectively by providing even more information proving that your solution will produce better results than your competitors.

Does that mean you will lose some leads? Inevitably, yes. Some of the people who come to you with a question will have that question answered, and they will walk away. However, if you help clarify their problems for them and clue them into the solution, then some of them will seek that solution elsewhere.

Much of the time, however, this is not the case. In fact, more often than not, if you are the one to answer your lead's questions and speak to the high value of your particular solution, those leads will move through your sales funnel and become not only customers but *loyal* customers who stick around for the long haul. Know that very few people are true "Do it Yourselfers," they just want to know you're the right person to do it for them.

This is also an opportune step in the process to remind them of WIIFM: "What's in it for me?" Remember that your prospects are not coming to you to hear how wonderful your business is. They are coming to you to learn more about themselves and how they can better their lives. If you start selling them immediately, all you do is prove you're in it for you. You need to prove instead that you are in it for *them*. If you provide something of value for free, then people are more willing to reciprocate.

That's really what personal branding is all about: proving that you have the consumer's best interest at heart. I hope that you take away from all this that your personal brand must exude not only confidence in the products and services you offer but that you have a strong ability to provide a solution to their problem, even if that's for free. If you can do this, you'll win big!

Now armed with a factual basis for understanding how to generate trust, and a blueprint for creating the reputation you want others to see online, you now have a compass to explore and leverage the hidden concepts behind affinity audiences, attraction marketing, and cause-based selling in a cohesive way. Through this illumination, if you dedicate yourself to incorporate these tactics into your marketing and branding efforts, you will get there.

Your success is rooted in being the best version of you, visible for the whole world to see. Now you are now faced with a critical decision point that could change the course of your life forever. You can choose between languishing in continued obscurity, living paycheck to paycheck, working from one barely profitable client to the next, or act now to start creating a powerful, trust-based business that will bring you endless profitable customers for long into the future, creating the business you have always dreamed of.

Which path will you choose?

About Matt Bertram

Matt Bertram is a trainer, author, local keynote speaker and consultant in Digital Marketing and Social Selling. He is currently the Co-host of the most popular SEO Podcast on iTunes and Ahrefs. He is COO at eWebResults, a top internet marketing agency since 1999.

As a lead Digital Marketing Strategist, Matt has led online marketing programs in Web Design, Sales Funnels, Search Engine Optimization (SEO), Pay-Per-Click Advertising (PPC), Social Media Marketing Strategy, and Recruiting Strategies.

He currently manages over $1.8 million in advertising dollars for clients.

Matt is a Google Partner with Google AdWords, Mobile, YouTube, Shopping, and Analytics Certifications, and has a strong track record of creating positive ROI with paid advertising for clients in a variety of different verticals. He has also consulted in the area of online personal branding for C-levels, Sales Directors, Realtors, and MLM Professionals.

As a Digital Marketing Trainer and certified personal consultant, Matt Bertram has co-developed workshops in the areas of SEO Basics, Advanced SEO Marketing Techniques, Social Selling, PPC and more.

Also, Matt is a Talent Acquisition Professional with over ten years of experience in sourcing and recruiting for positions for startup to Fortune 100 technology companies mainly in oil and gas and healthcare sectors through cold market strategies.

Matt is an expert in the development of near-term recruitment strategies to source and attract, screen, and select the most qualified candidates for difficult-to-fill positions.

If you are looking to grow your business or hire – use the largest, simplest marketing tool on the planet: the INTERNET!

Call **(281) 766-4550** for increased revenue in your business.

Schedule a FREE Consultation with Matt Today!
BuildYourBrandMania.com/consultation

You can also connect with Matt on the following platforms:

TWITTER
Twitter.com/MattBertramLive

LINKEDIN
LinkedIn.com/in/MattBertramLive

QUORA
Quora.com/profile/Matt-Bertram-5

 P.S. Check out "The Unknown Secrets of Internet Marketing" SEO Podcast on Podomatic, Stitcher, or iTunes.

Works Cited

Anton, G. (2018, January 29). *4 Reasons To Revitalize Your Email Marketing Strategy* . Retrieved from CMO.com: https://www.cmo.com/opinion/articles/2018/1/4/chec k-your-inbox-4-reasons-to-revitalize-your-email-strategy-in-2018.html#gs.qAREnMs

Baldwin, C. (2015, September 8). *Oak Furniture Land's email marketing revenue increases 30% due to geo-targeting.* Retrieved from Essential Retail: https://www.essentialretail.com/news/55ef07ab99d16 -oak-furniture-lands-email-marketing-revenue-increases-30-due-to-geo-targeting/

Dimensional Research. (2013, April). *The impact of customer service on customer lifetime value.* Retrieved from ZenDesk.com: https://www.zendesk.com/resources/customer-service-and-lifetime-customer-value/

Edelman Trust Barometer. (2012, January 23). *2012 Edelman Trust Barometer.* Retrieved from Edelman Trust Barometer Archive: https://www.edelman.com/2012-edelman-trust-barometer

Hubspot. (n.d.). *Marketing Benchmarks from 7,000+ Businesses.* Retrieved from Hubspot.com:

https://offers.hubspot.com/marketing-benchmarks-from-7000-businesses

Kilbourn, C. (2014, March 20). *Remarketing 101: A Beginner's Guide*. Retrieved from Search Engine Journal: https://www.searchenginejournal.com/remarketing-101-beginners-guide/89043/

Leszczynski, M. (2016, February 15). *The State of Email Marketing by Industry*. Retrieved from GetResponse.com: https://blog.getresponse.com/the-state-of-email-marketing-by-industry.html

Level Up Marketing. (n.d.). *Bedford Accountants Project*. Retrieved from Level Up Marketing: http://levelupmarketing.co.uk/digital-marketing-case-studies/bedford-accountants/

LinkedIn. (2014, October 24). *B2B Content Marketing Report*. Retrieved from LinkedIn: https://www.slideshare.net/hschulze/b2b-content-marketing-report-40688285

Margaret C. Wardle, D. A. (2013, June 20). *The Caudate Signals Bad Reputation during Trust Decisions*. Retrieved from PLOS One: http://journals.plos.org/plosone/article?id=10.1371/journal.pone.0068884

MDG Advertising. (2014, October 16). *MGDAvertising.com*. Retrieved from How Much Do Consumers Buy into Online Reviews?: https://www.mdgadvertising.com/marketing-insights/how-much-do-consumers-buy-into-online-reviews/

Michael Kosfeld, M. H. (2005, April 20). *Oxytocin increases trust in humans*. Retrieved from Nature International Journal of Science:

https://www.nature.com/articles/nature03701?foxtrotc
allback=true

Nancy L. Etcoff, S. S. (2011, October 3). *Cosmetics as a Feature of the Extended Human Phenotype: Modulation of the Perception of Biologically Important Facial Signals.* Retrieved from Plos One: http://journals.plos.org/plosone/article?id=10.1371/jo urnal.pone.0025656

Ouimet, M. (2013, July 12). *The secrets of Obama's email marketing success: Q&A with Toby Fallsgraff.* Retrieved from Oracle Modern Marketing Blog : https://blogs.oracle.com/marketingcloud/the-secrets-of-obamas-e-mail-success-qa-with-toby-fallsgraff

Oxytocin shapes the neural circuitry of trust and trust adaptation in humans. . (2008, May 22). Retrieved from PubMed.gov: https://www.ncbi.nlm.nih.gov/pubmed/18498743

Schweitzer, J. R. (2005). Feeling and Believing: The Influence of Emotion on Trust. *Journal of Personality and Social Psychology*, 745.

Statista. (2016). *Distribution of global social content sharing activities as of 2nd quarter 2016, by social network.* Retrieved from Statista: https://www.statista.com/statistics/283889/content-sharing-primary-social-networks-worldwide/

think with Google. (2013, May). *Loews Hotels Grows Customer Base with Similar Audiences.* Retrieved from think with Google: https://www.thinkwithgoogle.com/marketing-resources/loews-hotel-similar-audiences/

wishpond. (n.d.). *Ad Retargeting Statistics: Audience vs. Marketers Perspective.* Retrieved from wishpond: https://blog.wishpond.com/post/97571502803/infogra phic-ad-retargeting-statistics-audience

Zhel, M. (2016, May 9). *Email Marketing vs Social Media.* Retrieved from MailMunch.co: https://www.mailmunch.co/blog/email-marketing-vs-social-media/